LIFE AFTER DEATH
- LIVING PROOF

by
Tom Harrison

A Lifetime's Experiences
including
The Definitive Record
of the Remarkable
Physical Mediumship
of Minnie Harrison

from the weekly diaries and recorded notes of
her son Tom Harrison, Founder Manager of the
Arthur Findlay College, Stansted Hall

*A Record of Rare Physical Phenomena -
Apports - Trumpet and Direct Voice –
Full Ectoplasmic Materialisations*

First Edition

© Tom Harrison
2004

Published by
Saturday Night Press Publications

ISBN 0-9514534-1-6

Dedication

To my mother,
the dedicated members of the Saturday Night Club,
our inspirers and helpers from the Spirit World
and especially to my wife Ann
for her love, patience
and expertise in formulating this book.

Acknowledgements

I am greatly indebted to a host of friends for their help and support; in
particular to my close friend Eric Boyd for
his guidance during the early days of putting it all together;
to Chris Eldon Lee for allowing us to use some of his interviews; to
Katie Halliwell and the Stewart Alexander Circle for letting us
include material from their educational project;
to Malcolm Bruce-Radcliffe for his editing expertise ;
to David Haith for his journalistic advice;
and to David Fontana for his encouragement, over a number of years,
to write this book.

WELCOMED HOME

Sydney and Gladys Shipman were looking forward to
celebrating Sydney's 100th birthday on 5th March 2004
but sadly, after many months of gradual deterioration
in health, he passed quietly to the World of Spirit on
February 2nd 2004 – Gladys' 88th birthday.

He soon made contact with his wife and, although
his physical presence will be greatly missed, we know
he will soon be leading a very active life still advancing
the truth of Life after Death
a subject he has always pursued with great enthusiasm.
This quotation was one of his favourite maxims and I
feel that it encapsulates the ethic of this book.

"The with-holding of large truths from the world
may be a betrayal of the greatest trust."
Footfalls on the Boundary of Another World
by Robert Dale Owen

Contents

List of Illustrations

Foreword

This is a remarkable book by a remarkable man. Tom Harrison is one of those very rare individuals who have been privileged to witness, over a number of years, and in conditions that effectively rule out the possibility of trickery, some of the most amazing séance room phenomena reported since the days of D. D. Home and Eusapia Paladino. As reported by Tom in his book, these phenomena included ectoplasm, materialisations, conversations with spirits, apports, and touches by spirit hands, all of these things taking place in good light and in close proximity to the sitters.

At the time when these events took place, Tom was a young man; recently back from active service as an army officer in the Second World War. Trained as he was in accurate observation by his military experiences, he was able to keep careful notes of all that took place. I have read through these notes, all in Tom's own handwriting in the pages of his old army field notebook - the only paper available to him at the time, and they provide us with a fascinating first-hand record of evidence for the kind of paranormal phenomena that can occur within an intimate home circle of family members and friends sitting in the presence of an outstanding medium.

In addition to his notes, Tom's memory of everything that happened - as I know from many long conversations with him - is undimmed. So his book stands as an invaluable account of all that he experienced, sitting each week throughout the years from 1946 to 1955 with a home circle bound together by a deep commitment to contact what they considered to be the spirit world. I wonder if, in these hectic materialistic days, when families are far more likely to gather together around the television set than in the séance room, we will ever again see the like of such a circle.

For many of us, the events described in this book may sound miraculous, but for Tom there was no miracle about them. They were simply part of the facts of life. This is evident from the title of his first book, *Visits By Our Friends from the Other Side*, because for Tom and the other members of his circle - his wife Doris, his parents and close friends Sid and Gladys Shipman and Dr. Brittain Jones - the weekly séances in which they took part were simply an opportunity for meeting deceased loved ones, as natural to them as coming together in any family gathering. Natural because Tom was brought up in a home in which survival of physical death and the ability to communicate between this world and the next were accepted as a matter of course.

One of Tom's aunts, Agnes Abbott, was a celebrated medium. It was she indeed who brought Arthur Findlay, well-known for his books and for his gift of Stansted Hall to the Spiritualists' National Union, the evidence that convinced him beyond doubt that his mother lived after death (in his autobiography, *Looking Back*, Findlay tells us that he received no less than 92 correct - and no incorrect - facts through Agnes from his mother). Even more importantly, Tom's mother Minnie Harrison was an extraordinarily gifted physical medium, and it was she indeed who acted as medium for the home circle.

If she had sought publicity, Minnie Harrison would have been one of the sensations of the immediate post-war years. Her gifts, as described by Tom, were of the very highest order. Modest and unassuming, battling with serious ill-health, and in trance for most of the séances so that she rarely witnessed the phenomena herself, Minnie

Harrison facilitated each week the materialisations not only of Agnes Abbott (in the spirit world herself by this time), but of many other family members and friends well-known to the sitters.

The presence of a well-qualified scientist in the home circle, Dr. Brittain Jones, a Fellow of the Royal College of Surgeons and Medical Superintendent of Middlesbrough General Hospital - who was able to testify to the genuineness of the phenomena, lends extra credibility to Tom's record of events. In addition, all the sittings were held in Sid and Gladys Shipman's living room, a small room behind their baker's shop, and secure from the accomplices whose involvement would have been necessary were fraud to have taken place. Furthermore, there was no space *in* the room for anyone to move freely around, and no chance that Minnie Harrison could have slipped out of the improvised cabinet (a curtain across one corner of the room) week after week for nearly ten years and succeeded in impersonating a wide range of spirits in front of her family and close friends - and in a good light. In any case, Tom tells us that some of the spirits did not retreat behind the curtain after making their appearance, but gradually sank towards the floor before disappearing, as if through a non-existent trap door.

I initially learnt of Tom Harrison's home circle when I read a small advertisement for his first book, *Visits by Our Friends from the Other Side,* all proceeds of which are donated to charity. My interest in psychical research goes back to boyhood, and over the years I have been fortunate, partly through my involvement in the Society for Psychical Research, in having many direct experiences of apparently paranormal phenomena. Thus I am always interested in adding to the 500 or so books I have on the subject, and I sent for a copy of Tom's book. I was impressed by the honesty of the writing, and not long afterwards, seemingly quite by chance, Tom and I met. Thus began a close friendship and my knowledge of the man more than bears out the impression I gained from reading his first book.

He is a man of transparent integrity, with no ambition for personal status or reward. His only interest in recounting the experiences he had with his home circle is to share with us the total conviction these experiences have given him of the reality of life after death. This conviction has left him with a deep humility and a spiritual presence that endears him to all those who meet him. Together with many others, I have long been urging Tom to write a fuller account of his experiences, and I am delighted that at last he has consented to do so, and thus to give us the benefit not only of learning from them but from his gentle, abiding wisdom.

Why is the kind of physical phenomena described by Tom of such importance? Physical mediumship, although at one time central to the investigations by many of the most illustrious psychical researchers like Sir William Crookes, Sir William Barrett, and Dr. Alfred Russel Wallace (discoverer with Darwin of the theory of evolution), has gradually fallen into disfavour, principally because of charges of fraud and malpractice leveled against some physical mediums. In addition the number of good physical mediums has declined sharply over the years (though there are now signs that this decline may at last be halted and even reversed).

So why should we still be concerned about physical phenomena? The answer is that, provided the spirits responsible for these phenomena can convince sitters they are who they say they are, and that the conditions discount the possibility of fraud, physical phenomena provides us with paranormal events of a range and a strength that have never been duplicated by living beings, whatever their psychic abilities. This weakens the argument that all evidence for survival produced by mediumship can be dismissed on the grounds that the medium could be obtaining her information through her own powers of telepathy and clairvoyance. I know of no reliable evidence that the living can produce the range and extent of phenomena witnessed in the context of physical mediumship. Read Tom's book, and draw your own conclusions.

We thus have every reason to be grateful to Tom Harrison, firstly for keeping records of the events at his home circle, and secondly for sharing these records with us. And we have equal reason to be grateful to the late Minnie Harrison and to the other members of his home circle, five of them no longer with us in this world, who dedicated so much of their time and energies to meeting each week in order to provide evidence of life after death. Tom's book is full of extraordinary examples of this evidence, and equally full of his· own warmth and humanity. As I said at the outset, a remarkable book by a remarkable man. Thank you Tom.

Professor David Fontana

Former President Society for Psychical Research

December 2003

Preface - Welcome to my world

Death is nothing at all......
I have only slipped away into the next room.........

What is this death but a negligible accident?
Why should I be out of mind because I am out of sight?
I am waiting for you, for an interval,
Somewhere, very near, just around the corner.
All is well.   *(Canon Henry Scott Holland)*

Welcome to the World of Spirit, the so-called 'next world', an all-pervading world of which we are all a part – here and now. This physical body is nothing more than a transient shell to clothe the individual living Spirit during its momentary existence on this material globe known as the Earth.

When this body has reached its 'sell by' date and serves no further useful purpose, however and whenever that may occur, the individual Spirit, the 'real you' within that body, will simply continue to live on in the World of Spirit, but freed from the encumbrance of this restrictive 'suit of clay'. Personal freedom and unrestricted joy will be yours in the wondrous, very real, world of pristine beauty on a much finer vibration. Analogous, perhaps, but in a much more refined and resplendent manner, to the transition of the delicate, beautiful butterfly from the 'leaf-locked' caterpillar via the restrictive shell of the chrysalis. That caterpillar retains its 'individuality' through to the butterfly, in the same way as you will retain your individuality when you pass to the Spirit World.

Never forget that your loved ones, relatives and friends, will be waiting to welcome you when you make that transition and they are anxious to let you know they are still close to you, never more than a thought away. Like those intuitive thoughts we often receive that someone is going to telephone us and within a moment or two the bell rings and they are on the line chatting to us. If only we used that 'intuition' more often to listen to our loved ones from the World of Spirit, how much happier all parts of the Spirit World would be. I am reminded of one of those 'trick ' questions at school —"Which was the largest continental island before Australia was discovered"? After all our replies were negated the master simply said, with a chuckle, that the answer was still that landmass, now known as Australia. Before it was discovered, it had always been there!

So for 'Australia' please read 'Spirit World' – it has always been there and I am so pleased to say that more and more people are beginning to know more about it and make contact, much to the delight of our friends in the Spirit World. The one certainty about this life here is that we will ALL 'die' and make that journey to the world of Spirit, irrespective of nationality or religious beliefs. How splendid it would be if the travel agents had coloured illustrated brochures to cover that unique very special journey – as they do for all the other distant journeys we like to make to 'foreign parts' – so that we have some idea of our destination. Unfortunately such brochures are not available, but the KNOWLEDGE about our destination IS AVAILABLE – if only 'humanity' took the time and trouble to seek in the right places, so often within themselves.

From a personal aspect I have been privileged to be aware of this knowledge from an early age, and even more privileged to have access to the means of making contact with so many people in the Spirit World. This awareness was so absolute that, when I had to give my religion on entering the Army I could say, without a doubt, I was a

Spiritualist. Experiences throughout my life have brought me to the understanding that this knowledge is beyond the label of a specific religion and as I have said belongs and applies to all of mankind. The message which Douglas gives in the Christmas Party Sitting, to 'follow the Christ Principle' of love for others is so fundamental to our life that we need to rise above the divisions of sectarianism and religion. Throughout my life I have been privileged in so many ways, but none more so than those concerning the Spirit World. Such privileges are indeed a joy to be treasured and nurtured for the benefit of mankind whenever or wherever an opportunity presents itself. Forget not however that all Privileges carry the Personal Responsibility to accept and use them with the greatest Humility, without which our quality and dignity of life would be diminished.

1

Living Proof - The Evidence.

"How do I begin to tell the story of so great a love ..."

For overwhelming tangible love is the emotion, which is felt when they return.

This is a story almost too unbelievable to relate.

All your senses will resist believing it.

You are being asked to accept that people returned from the dead - not as fleeting passing visions in somebody's mind, not even as wispy transparent ghosts or spectres.

But they returned in fully functioning, warm, heart-beating physical bodies.

They returned and spoke with the same sounding voices you recognise.

They returned with the same laughter, the same personality and, as you thrilled to feel their arms embracing you and even kisses from their lips - the same love.

Yes, you will resist believing it.

But I know it happened. I was there. I met these real people, materialised from the world beyond death, hundreds and hundreds of times. And I have the written records, the tape recordings, the photographs, the solid objects - 'gifts' teleported through the dimensions, as evidence.

And then, when you still resist believing the unbelievable, I'll introduce you to the witnesses - the people from all walks of life who for eight long years also

met the 'living' dead at the experimental séances we called
The Saturday Night Club.

It all happened in a tiny back room of a small house in
Middlesbrough, UK where our family sat weekly for a
'Home Circle'.

My mother Minnie Harrison was undoubtedly
the unique focus of our cosmic breakthrough,
which unlocked the dimensional doorway to the other side.

It was with use of her psychic ability and through her
body that the mysterious substance known as ectoplasm
flowed to form the beings we recognised as our 'lost' loved
ones.

Such experiences, woven into my life from a very early
age, have been life changing for the scores of 'guest sitters'
at our weekly gatherings, including Roy, Gwen, Don and
Emily who below, each give 'tasters' of their
incredible encounters with those who physically returned
from beyond death.

Roy Dixon Smith, retired Lt. Colonel, a complete stranger,
who, in 1948, made the train journey from London to
Middlesbrough expressly to spend an hour or so with us in
our Home Circle, where, in a good red light, he met,
conversed with, held hands with, looked closely into the
eyes of and finally kissed the fully materialised,
ectoplasmic, form of his beloved wife Betty who had passed
to Spirit some four years earlier. He was so convinced that
he and Betty had been re-united and that the other Spirit
people he met were absolutely 'real', he wrote a chapter in
his book 'New Light on Survival', an excerpt of which I
have included in this book.

Gwen Schlegel, a well educated lifelong Middlesbrough
resident, who was so enthralled and convinced by her visit
to our Home Circle in 1954, accompanied by her mother,
she willingly agreed to broadcast her knowledge far and
wide on the BBC Radio 4 programme 'Christmas Spirits' in

December 2003. She told the listeners in a compelling and articulate manner --

"I know without a shadow of doubt that there is life after death. There is no question about it –such a comfort – I know my loved ones are waiting for me. Before the sitting started I was terrified, but after it started, to my astonishment, into the room in a full red light came this little old lady. She was absolutely fantastic. She was jolly and friendly and full of fun.

She came to each of us in turn and shook our hands and welcomed us. At that moment all my fears left me. I saw her face clearly, very clearly. She was in like a white shroud – the ectoplasm. Her face was a human face, lovely smile, laughing eyes. It was an old lady's hand I took hold of, warm, like meeting a living person. I just wish everyone knew this".

"After the old lady had gone, my mother's sister Aunt Jane came. She was amazing. She had been dead a couple of years and this was her first time to materialise. She found it very difficult - unable to draw herself to her full height but I clearly recognised her. All the time I had known her she had been deaf and dumb but she was very excited tonight to be able to speak to her sister Phoebe by name. She said it slowly like 'Pheeeee….beeee'. I remember that so vividly – it was the first time I had heard her speak. It was all so amazing, in a red light. Everything could be clearly seen. I'll never forget it as long as I live. I was there. They hugged us. We held hands. It was amazing."

"I can fully understand people who think this is all crazy. I would have done so, but now I have seen it and know otherwise".

Gwen was also thrilled to be given an apported carnation to take home with her. The 'little old lady' was Granny Lumsden, my wife's grandmother, one of our regular Spirit visitors who has a separate chapter to herself.

Don McKenzie - a retired electrical engineer, who helped his father set up the recording equipment for our 'one-off' recorded Christmas party sitting in January 1954 and then stayed for his first sitting, as a young man of 19. He, like Gwen, was so impressed by what he saw that he had no difficulty in recalling the events of that evening when interviewed fifty years later for the same 'Christmas Spirits' broadcast.

"I saw a materialised form build up and come out of the cabinet. I actually went across and shook hands with one of the regular Spirit people who came, because they build up quite strongly. A wonderful experience – actual proof to me – I shook hands and talked to this old lady. Quite firm. An important thing in my life."

'Could it have been faked?' asked the Programme Producer, "No way at all. We were allowed to go into the room before it started and have a look round – an ordinary room in a domestic house. There could be no other explanation, when you actually see the materialised form come out from the cabinet. The medium was a plump tallish lady – and you see a slim Spirit form standing there erect to shake hands with you. No way can that be faked"

In addition to all the other materialisation phenomena that night, Don also saw his brother Bruce materialise. Bruce spoke with Don and his mother and father but was not strong enough to stand their touch. Don also heard, through the 'trumpet', the voices of his mother's mother, Margaret Phoenix, and Margaret McKenzie, his father's grandmother who all spoke to him. His father was very excited, because for the first time ever he had her typical Scottish accent on tape.

"We were very privileged to witness what the regular sitters saw every week. To see, hear, touch and feel – an experience that remains with you for the rest of your life. Even now 50 years later I still remember it."

Emily Nicholson's visit as a guest sitter in the late 1940's was recounted to me by her daughter, Mary Hastie, then in her late sixties, after one of my talks at Billingham Church in May 1996.

Mary told me that her mother never stopped talking about it, it had meant so much to her. During the sitting her stepmother, Polly, materialised and stepped out of the cabinet. She came up to Emily, who put out her hand to shake hands with her, but Polly brushed away her hand and said, "We don't shake hands'" – then clasped Emily in her arms in a loving hug – which was warm and solid to her. There was an overwhelming pouring of love from Polly to Mum. It was a truly wonderful experience for her – one she never forgot. Later in the sitting she received an apport of a carnation, which she treasured for years.

These are only four of the 200+ guest sitters, whose experiences were all similar – unforgettable, very personal, exciting contacts with loving Spirit people they knew and clearly recognised.

'All faked' is the usual dismissive remark of the sceptic – 'Any magician could do it. You've been conned'. Really?

I am absolutely certain that no magician, stripped of his equipment, sitting alone on a dining chair in a small room in a strange house, where it was not possible to open the door without someone having to stand up, and in full view of the assembled sitters, as my mother was, could produce anything resembling the wonderful materialisations we met and conversed with, week after week after week for so many years.

And then I simply ask you - what purpose would faking have served? There was certainly no motive – financial or otherwise – no charge was ever made, my mother abhorred the very thought, and all guests partook of Gladys' supper afterwards.

Even if she had had the ability or facilities, why would my mother desire to deceive her husband, my wife and me and two very close friends, Syd and Gladys Shipman, at whose home she arrived by bus, only a few minutes before we had our sitting. My mother was certainly not devious. She was humble, amiable, unpretentious and loving. Keen to help those in need, she always gave freely of her remarkable gift. She sacrificed her time every week for the benefit of others.

I believe I am a reasonably perceptive man with my 7 years Army service training behind me and I am completely convinced that all those 1,500+ solid materialised Spirit people, seen and met in good red light – were whom they said they were. I knew my mother's sister, Aunt Agg, very closely indeed; had stayed and lived with her on numerous occasions, a kind and gentle lady. I had no doubt whatsoever that the materialised person who came almost every week was that same lady who had passed over in 1942. My father, Doris and Sydney, who also knew her well, were of exactly the same mind. Likewise, Doris and her mother Annie (nee Lumsden), a frequent guest sitter, were completely convinced that 'the materialised lively little old lady', who came so often, as described by Gwen, was truly their Granny Lumsden who passed over in 1930.

You will hear more of these people and many others, as the book proceeds. All I ask is that you keep an open mind and enjoy the true intriguing accounts of such joyful reunions.

This joy is also evident in the poem, 'WE LIVE', composed in 1954, by my Uncle Jack Bessant, my mother's brother who was killed in a works accident in 1927. I was delighted and privileged to write it down as he spoke to us through the mediumship of my mother who was in deep trance – completely 'asleep' and oblivious to her surroundings.

We Live!

Mourn not for me my loved ones, for I am by your side,
I have not sped to realms unknown
or crossed the rolling tide.
I do not leave you comfortless, think not I ever will.
So dry those tears, look up and smile, for I am with you still.

My eyes once closed are opened, my vision clear and bright,
Where once I looked through darkened glass,
I see perpetual light.
The veil has just been lifted and my loved ones gone before
Are waiting now to welcome me, as in the days of yore.

Their love is still enfolding me; their Spirits have not fled,
And now I know as I am known.
WE LIVE! There are no dead.
So let your hearts be comforted, cast out all doubt and fear,
We live and walk beside you – your loved ones still are near.

Grieve not for me my dear ones, just dry those tears away;
I'll walk with you through Earth's dark night
until the break of day.
So lift your hearts in thankful praise and join with us to sing –
O Grave, where is thy victory?
O Death, where is thy sting?

~~~~~

Minnie Rose Harrison – My Mother
1942

2

My Mother – Minnie Rose Harrison

Minnie Rose was born on 17th March 1895 in Middlesbrough. She was the youngest of 11 children in the Bessant family.

Her father was a sugar boiler and confectioner and the family lived, at various times, in Middlesbrough and the Bristol area. Her mother died when she was only five years old. Her father married his wife's sister to help him with the family and so into our family came the lady affectionately known as Auntie-Grandma.

Whilst the family were living in Bristol, Albert, the eldest of the family and 23 years older than my mother, was sent as a delegate to a Salvation Army Conference in York. As he was getting into bed in his lodgings the candle was blown out; he lit it again and again it was blown out. A little un-nerved he got into bed only to have the covers pulled off his bed. We don't know what kind of a night he spent but on his return to Bristol he was telling a workmate about his experiences and his friend suggested he talk to one of his friends who was a Spiritualist.

The discussion led to an invitation to a Home Circle and the eventual development of the whole family. Parental encouragement enabled them to develop in an uninhibited environment and from her teenage years my mother had been both clairvoyant and clairaudient. In varying degrees all the children were mediumistic. Four of them, Jack, Mary, Agnes and my mother, Minnie, developed into deep-control trance mediums.

When my mother was in her 'teens, a few years before World War I, her family lived in Union Street, Middlesbrough, next door to a blind gentleman Mr Bartle. She used to tell of how she and one of her sisters used to creep into his house to try to surprise him, but he always knew they were there - his hearing was so acute. They used to talk about life after death, but Mr Bartle could not really accept it. He did however make a promise to my mother - "If there is anything in your beloved Spiritualism Minnie, when I have gone I will come back and let you know." Shortly after his promise, Mr Bartle passed over and his promise slipped into the background.

When one of her elder sisters, Mary, married and moved to Bristol, my mother, now in her late 'teens, would go to stay with her for holidays. While she was there she would walk around the centre of the city, exploring many of the narrow side streets. It was on one of these walks she happened to see a small notice about a Spiritualist church above a shop, as so many of them were then. My mother was intrigued. She climbed the stairs, entered the room and sat at the back.

The service had started and the medium was a lady completely unknown to my mother, in a city which she visited only very occasionally. Messages from Spirit people were given to a few of the congregation before the medium finally came to my mother. The message was very brief but quite startling. She described a gentleman, standing alongside my mother, telling her he had been blind and said he just wanted to say to her - "*Yes Minnie, there is something in your beloved Spiritualism*".

She was, of course, thrilled to receive such remarkable evidence and never forgot that Mr Bartle had kept his promise made some years previously. As far as I know that was the only contact with him, but it was certainly sufficient to authenticate my mother's belief that there was life after death - as was proven through her remarkable mediumship over 30 years later.

My mother married my father, Thomas Henry Harrison in April 1915, during the World War I, and lived with her father and his second wife in Middlesbrough, whilst 'Tosher' was away in France, fighting, and where he was 'gassed' by the mustard gas' which affected him for the rest of his life.

When I was very young, to help spin out the small wage my father got with the railways, my mother worked in the small sub-post office and general store belonging to Mr and Mrs Cowell Pugh. They were staunch Spiritualists, acting as hosts to Billy Hope and Mrs Buxton when they went to Middlesbrough to take the photographs of local people that often contained Spirit 'extras'. Several of the family had photos taken and I still have this precious record.

During the mid-1920s, whilst we were living in Shakespeare Street my mother started her first 'home-made toffee' shop, a business, which continued for many years in our various houses, all near to schools. Her father taught three of his children his 'trade secrets'. My Uncle Toss and Aunt Agg were the other two, and both had successful confectionery businesses in Middlesbrough for a number of years. Our house, immediately facing the entrance to the schoolyard, was ideally situated to attract the children's ha'pennies and pennies on their way to and from school. They had several choices, including 'mint rock', 'aniseed twist', nut toffee, 'pear drops' made by passing the almost-set toffee through indented brass rollers etc., but the regular favourite, at one penny a quarter of a pound, was 'treacle' toffee made from my mother's special secret mix of brown sugars, with a pinch of cream of tartar to stop it going 'claggy' in damp weather. When suitable sized apples were available, toffee apples were also very popular.

With her inherent love of children, she considered her regular' customers' almost as family and in her usual unobtrusive way gave them surprise treats by having some of the bags marked with a lucky 'T', stuck on the inside, which entitled them to a free bag of toffee the next day. She always made sure the lucky 'T' bag, kept in a separate pile from the others, went to deserving children. Mam was well ahead of today's 'prize in the pack' promotions.

On Saturdays, to supplement our income, Mam, Dad and I with one of our many friends, used to take a stall selling toffee at the local markets in Stockton, South Bank or Redcar. I well remember 'shouting the odds' to attract passers-by to buy our home made toffee and there were quite a large number of regular satisfied customers who gave me a kind word, a smile and sometimes an extra ha'penny or penny for myself. I could, sometimes, find myself going home with as much as sixpence in my pocket. What wealth for a 10 year old! One of the highlights of those days for me was when I was allowed to break up the toffee slabs with the attractive little metal hammers. Great fun that was! The trays of toffee were carried in two or three metal trunks that we transported on the local buses. Busy and exciting days they were and although in the winter when it was pouring with rain or the roads covered with snow and ice, we usually managed to get there. Those were the days when to wrap your freezing fingers round a mug of hot Bovril from a nearby tea stall was sheer bliss - at a penny a time!

I find it difficult to believe how my mother managed to boil all that sugar on the tiny gas cooker we had; how my father made a small 'window shelf' and serving counter for use in the very small living room of our rented house, both of which had to be dismantled each evening to make room for the many folk who visited us. We had an ever-open door for friends and relatives, many of whom were unemployed, and in retrospect I feel sure that Mam used a lot of the money from the shop to feed and help them all. But that was typical of my mother's philosophy and generosity throughout her life. She would deny herself for the benefit of others, as she did when Doris and I were bringing up our family of three boys and three girls. I only discovered this after her passing - but she would not have wanted it any other way.

In the late 1930's Aunt Agg, who was ten years older than my mother, and already working as a professional medium at the Marylebone Spiritualist Association, recommended her for acceptance to work there as a medium. She passed all the 'test sittings' in London but eventually she decided not to join Aunt Agg and stayed in Middlesbrough. The money they received for sittings in London must have been very tempting for someone struggling through the Depression, but I believe it was that aspect which swung her decision, because she could never bring herself to make any charge for her sittings. No guest to our Saturday Night Club was ever charged anything —my mother abhorred the idea, irrespective of her personal limited finances.

From her teenage years, together with her brothers and sisters, my mother had been an active member of the Lyceum, the Sunday-School section of the Spiritualists National Union and had become close friends with Charles and Annie Hudson who were staunch supporters and workers for the Middlesbrough Spiritualist Church. Doris, the second eldest of their family of ten was a favourite with my mother and she made sure we got to know each other very well. My mother was popular as a medium around the local churches and would travel, with Sydney Shipman, to take services. Sydney had developed as a good speaker on the Philosophical aspect of Spiritualism and my mother gave the contact with those from the Spirit World.

I well remember in later years when I was 'chairing' the meetings at Middlesbrough Church how nervous my mother would be, afraid that no Spirit would communicate. As soon as she stood to give that contact with the spirit World she would go into the sleep like state of deep trance and her sister, Agg, would control her and give all the contacts for the people there; trance-clairvoyance, again a rare form of mediumship.

The anticipated pleasure of becoming grandparents helped my mother's recovery, following her operation for cancer in 1940. But it rather had the edge taken off it when our firstborn decided to arrive. As soon as Doris realised the time of the birth was only a few days away, my parents moved in with her to give any help that might be needed.

In the early hours of the morning of the 23rd of February 1942, Dad was on messenger duty. He telephoned the midwife and went to let Doris's mother know, who then hurried round to our house. Since the previous evening snow had been falling in Middlesbrough; now it was more than a foot deep, and still falling. The midwife was not able to cycle the two miles to our home in Lambeth Road. Midwives did not have the luxury of cars in those days.

When the midwife did not arrive Doris's midwifery skills had to take over. Although Mrs Hudson had had 10 children, neither she nor my mother had ever seen a baby born - so now was their time to learn! Under Doris's detailed instructions, Colin was delivered safely. The midwife arrived shortly afterwards to do the 'tidying up'. It must have been quite a night for them all!

Through out the war, while I was away in the army my mother and father with Doris would go for their weekly Saturday visit to Sydney and Gladys Shipman's home, for a chat and musical evening, with Syd on the violin and Gladys accompanying him on the piano. Whenever I was home on leave, I would join them also. If I happened to be in the UK with my Unit, I would make every effort to get to a telephone box to ring Syd and Gladys and talk to Doris and my parents, who because of their shop had a telephone keeping a very important link between the six of us.

In March 1946, after I had been demobbed, we continued to enjoy the Saturday evening social visits to Syd and Gladys' home. It was only about three weeks later that Syd suggested we have a Home Circle - with which we all heartily agreed, never realising what remarkable results we would be privileged to receive over the next few years! Albert's statement at Helen Duncan's sitting almost nine years previously about the 'physical phenomena energy' certainly came true and my mother's mediumship amazed and astounded us all not only by the rapidity of its development but in its unexpected quality and rarity. The 6th April 1946 was the start of something unique and extremely special with the start of the Saturday Night Club.

Towards the end of 1946 Mam and I talked about the possibility of having a fish and chip shop to operate between us, with Dad still continuing his job in the railway goods yard. We had had no previous experience in such a business but fancied our chances. Within a few weeks a shop became available in Garnet Street and we decided to go for it.

Early in December we opened our fish and chip shop. Mam and Dad sold their Longford Street house - from which I had been married - and moved into the shop's living quarters later that month. A bit different from the toffee shops Mam had had over the years, but it proved quite successful and soon we were taking over £80 per week with a useful net profit - a big improvement on my old wages which made such a difference to our everyday living.

Eventually we sold the Garnet Street shop to some of her sister, Mary's, family from Bristol. Mam and Dad bought another Fish & Chip shop in Bow Street where they stayed for a number of years. As Dad's breathing problems worsened he left the railways and helped in the preparation of the fish and potatoes, while Mam and one of Uncle Toss's daughters Ethel, known to us all as 'our Eth', a very friendly and cheerful widow, ran the shop. As the cancer started to spread and her health worsened, they sold the shop and came to live with us in Oxford Road.

When we had the Circle, to help my mother relax into her trance state, after she had moved back into the cabinet for the materialisation phenomena, we always sang 'Silent

Night'. We usually sang about two verses before Sunrise spoke to us from the cabinet ready to commence the phenomena. During the lead-up to Christmas in 1948, Doris and my mother were doing some shopping in the town. They went into one of the cafés for a coffee. Christmas carols were being played through the speaker system, which Doris told us, was very pleasant until they played 'Silent Night'. Doris said that as soon as 'Silent Night' started my mother closed her eyes and appeared to be drifting into a trance state as she did during our sittings. She had sub-consciously been 'conditioned' by that tune and Doris had to quickly call her name quite a few times to bring her back to drink her coffee. We're not sure what would have happened if my mother had been on her own but we are quite sure she would not have come to any harm, Sunrise and Aunt Agg would have seen to that - but it might have been a little surprising for the other customers and embarrassing for my mother.

Following my mother's first operation for cancer in 1940, over the next eighteen years, she had several more minor operations and treatments which kept her going but sometimes the Specialists were baffled as to how she was keeping so well. They expressed as much saying to her 'Something is doing you more good than we can.' and Mr Jones, who was a personal friend of her surgeon, used to tell him about Sunrise and the value of Spirit healing!

During the weekly Circle sessions she received healing from the Spirit World while we sat, for which she was so thankful! This was confirmed by the fact that, because of the constant pain in her left arm particularly, she had sleepless nights - except on Saturday nights, after our sittings, when she had at least five hours unbroken sleep. After the mastectomy in 1940, her left arm had swollen considerably and she could lift it only a few inches from her side - until Sunrise took control, which he would do at the end of the trumpet phenomena part of the sitting.

When we switched on the red light for the second part of the circle and the materialisations, Sunrise often performed his unique 'healing miracle'. Speaking to us through my mother, he would stand her erect, slowly lift her left arm forward and then rapidly swing it round and round in a circular motion, saying at the same time: "I give Meedi healing" (he always referred to my mother as 'my Meedi'). This would last about a minute and he would then sit her down again ready to move into the cabinet behind her.

We never ceased to be impressed by the sight of mother's arm whirling round and round, when normally she could hardly move it. When we told her after the sitting, she found it very difficult to believe, but was ever grateful to Sunrise for all his help which allowed her to continue with what they both considered her important work for the Spirit World. The movement in her arm continued to be limited but it certainly did not deteriorate, as would have been expected according to the medical staff. As Sunrise said, on the Christmas Party tape recording in 1954, " We keep Meedi in good physical condition to do the work".

We knew the Spirit folk were always close around, particularly her sister, Agg, with whom she had had a special rapport and who communicated through her so easily but we had a very pleasant surprise one evening when my mother was in hospital following a minor operation to stop the cancer spreading. During one of these visits, Doris and I were allowed to sit by her bedside during the one hour visiting time before she had recovered from the anaesthetic, which we were told would be some time yet. The ward was full of other visitors making conversation with the patients while we sat quietly one each side of the bed, holding mother's hands to try to give her spiritual healing.

We quietly sat either side of her bed, holding her hands. We kept glancing towards her face and mid-way through the hour we were amazed, to see her, still with her eyes closed, smiling at us. She appeared to want to speak to us, so we leaned forward to try to listen above the surrounding hum. As we got close to her we both realised that it was Aunt Agg controlling her. "Aunt Agg?" I questioned. "Yes, I've just popped in to let you know Our Min will be all right. We are looking after her." With that she was gone and no one else on the busy ward was aware of what had happened. Little did all the visitors realise what we had just witnessed - a minor miracle under such difficult circumstances, but the extremely close empathy between the two sisters was evident once again.

Eventually the cancer worsened and was the cause of her passing to the Spirit World on November 7th 1958, aged 63. Her passing naturally left a huge gap in our lives. Apart from the physical loss for me of my mother and our children's loss of their loving 'Narnee', as they called her, we lost that wonderful regular physical contact with our family, friends and helpers in the Spirit World, which we had had for some 12 years. With her mediumistic gift and her caring nature, she had enhanced so many peoples' lives.

Although we continued to have a Home Circle, where some of the family developed mental and light trance control mediumship, the gift of my mother's extremely rare and wonderful mediumship was not evident in either myself or any of our six children, and the years of the Saturday Night club had reached their end. I have since, however, as a member of another splendid Home Circle talked with her and my father and felt my mother's touch and know that they are enjoying a happy life free from the pain and discomfort they experienced on Earth.

Thank you Mam for all the loving care you gave us and so many others.

Tom aged 3, with his mother and father.
1922

3

A few words about me ...

You are fully entitled to be wondering who I am, writing this extraordinary story about life after death. Am I an eccentric living a life of fantasy or am I just an ordinary fellow who has lived an ordinary but privileged life, experiencing unique manifestations of physical psychic phenomena through the remarkable mediumship of my mother, Minnie Harrison. I believe I am that ordinary, everyday man, but here is a brief resume of my life to enable you to reach your own decision. So here goes.

I was born in Middlesbrough, North Yorkshire, on the eighth of August 1918 at the height of the influenza pandemic, which was responsible for some 15 million deaths worldwide. My mother, at 23 years old, was left with a weakened heart, and I learned later that I was considered a 'sickly' boy during my early childhood. Such health conditions were overcome sufficiently to combat the years of the 'Depression' in that dark period between the two World Wars. My father served in the trenches throughout the World War I; was gassed and wounded in the leg on the Somme and was thankful to get a steady job as a checker with the North Eastern Railway.
His weekly wage was about two pounds, not a princely sum, but vastly better than the many thousands of unemployed in the North East who had little or no financial assistance. I must admit that I was too young to recall the effect of the worst of those years and was so

fortunate to have a loving secure home life as an only child.

In those days we lived in a rented very small two-up-two-down terraced house in Shakespeare Street, with the usual 'unfriendly' outside lavatory and coalhouse. Nobody we knew had the luxury of a bathroom, so Friday night was bath night in the zinc bathtub stood in front of the fireplace. Number 95 was opposite the back entrance to Victoria Road School, which, in spite of a few house moves, I attended until I was eleven years old and won a Scholarship to Middlesbrough High School. I always enjoyed mathematics and the sciences and managed to obtain a Matriculation Certificate in 1934. I realised I had no chance of going to university, as there were so few places available, and so in 1935 I was fortunate to obtain a job, in those difficult times, at seventeen shillings a week, as a junior clerk with a small new company established on the vast I.C.I. Tees-side site at Billingham. British Titan Products, later renamed Tioxide, is now a very large conglomerate with another large factory on South Humberside.

I enjoyed my school days, especially the sports activities – athletics, soccer and rugby – and obtained my 'school colours' –looked on as a great achievement in those days. Likewise I enjoyed my 4 years at B.T.P. including the 16 miles cycle ride to and from home each day until, in 1939, the Government decided to call up batches of 20 years-old as peace-time conscripts (the fore-runner to National Service), which resulted in me and two hundred others reporting to the Corps of Royal Engineers in Aldershot on the 15th July. We were to serve 6 months, with our jobs secured, but with the declaration of war on 3rd September, it lasted for the duration of World War II, which for me was almost 7 years. Again I count myself very fortunate to have what might be loosely termed a 'quiet' war with the accepted discomforts and concerns for my family back home.

But let me recount 3 significant happenings concerning Physical Psychic Phenomena, in the years before my Army service. We always had lots of friends calling on us, but there was one special evening each week when the same group of people met in the small living room in Shakespeare Street. I was no more than four years old at the time and used to enjoy listening to my mother playing the little harmonium in the corner of the living room whilst the assembled group of about seven friends heartily sang songs. I had no idea what it was all about but just enjoyed lying in bed listening before going to sleep. Until one night... I was awakened by a rather loud, strange voice coming from the room below. Inquisitive as always, I crept down the open staircase to investigate, and in the light of the dying embers, saw the group sitting round the fireplace, with mother's brother, Uncle Jack, standing up speaking in this strange voice. He was being 'controlled' by the Spirit of an African Chief who was his main Guide. Mam saw me on the stairs and beckoned me to go down and sit on her knee. I remember I did not feel at all afraid, rather quite at home, but don't recall much else as I must have quickly gone to sleep again and then been carried up to bed. This was my introduction to trance phenomena at an unusually early age.

My next special memory was when I was about 17 years old, spending a holiday with my parents at Aunt Agg's house in Cricklewood, London. Aunt Agg was a 'professional' medium with the MSA. - the Marylebone Spiritualist Association (later to become the S.A.G.B.) but still had her Home Circle as a 'trumpet' medium. Mam and Dad joined her circle but it meant nothing to me at that time so my cousin, Terry, and I went out to the local café. When we returned they were still sitting, so we went quietly into the kitchen and I made the comment that it was all a 'load of boloney'. A few minutes later they had finished and we were invited to join them in the sitting room. As we entered I repeated – 'it's all a load of boloney' and the sitters roared with laughter. Apparently one of

Aunt Agg's guides, Paddy, had just previously told them that the 'young gentleman say it all a load of boloney'! Little did I realise how wrong I was and how much I was to learn some 11 years later, about trumpet and other forms of physical phenomena, including materialisation in our Home Circle.

The most impressive memory however, was when at 19 years old, I was really privileged to sit in a Helen Duncan Materialisation Circle where my mother was the 'hostess' for a friend, Sam Ingham, in whose lounge the Circle was held. At the time I knew very little about materialisation but had read about it and was very interested. My mother was one of the ladies who did the usual 'strip search' of Helen before she put on the simple black shift ready for the sitting. They then stayed with her and accompanied her until she sat in the cabinet to ensure she was secreting nothing on her person. The room had been examined by other impartial sitters and Helen took her place on a simple dining chair behind the black curtain across the corner, adjacent to the fireplace.

The sitting was held in a dim red light and as I was seated in the back row of three I could not have described in detail the ectoplasmic Spirit people who stood in front of the cabinet, but they appeared very solid and were apparently recognised by different sitters nearer to them. Albert, Helen's main guide, acted as the 'Master of Ceremonies' and the whole evening was most enjoyable. But the highlight for my mother and me came with the last materialisation. It was my mother's brother Jack, who had been killed in a works accident about ten years previously, and whom I had heard speaking in trance that night, as I sat on my mother's knee.

He built very strongly, stayed about 4 minutes and spoke clearly to my mother who was in the front row. After he had moved back behind the curtain we could still hear him talking to Albert who then announced that the people whom that gentleman had come to contact, had the right energy for physical phenomena! Although my mother at that time was a good mental medium, it was difficult for us to fully comprehend such unexpected and significant information from such a reliable source. Little did we know that some 8 years later it would all come to pass as Albert had intimated during that very exciting evening with that very special medium, Helen Duncan.

From my early years I remember being taken by my mother every Sunday to the Lyceum Sunday School where I enjoyed both the friendship of so many children and listening to the interesting lessons about life in the Spirit World. It was there, in our early teens, that Doris and I met. Our friendship grew and I enjoyed being part of the Hudson family of ten children, who all attended the Lyceum. Our friendship blossomed into courtship and Doris and I were married on 2nd April 1940, in Middlesbrough Spiritualist Church, during my second leave from the British Expeditionary Force stationed in France. Nothing much of significance occurred during my service as a driver with the Field Survey mapping unit of the B.E.F., apart from my promotion from driver to Corporal clerk and it deservedly became known as the 'Bore War' – until the Germans rounded the French Maginot Line defences and, as we were not a fighting unit, we had to beat a hasty and unpleasant retreat through Dunkirk, making it on to almost the last boat to get out of the harbour.

As soon as we landed in Dover we were piled into a train and finished up in Llandudno, North Wales, where we stayed for 4 months before sailing from Glasgow to arrive, after 4 days rough sailing, in Iceland to do some mapping of the 'major' ports on the north and east coasts. We were stationed in the capital, Reykjavik, firstly in bell tents on frozen rough ground for about 2 months until Nissen huts were ready on spare land alongside our HQ offices on the waterfront.

I have a number of lasting impressions of our year's stay in Iceland, including the permanent sub-zero temperatures to which we remarkably quickly became acclimatised and the 'permanent nights' during the winter months when the maximum daylight we saw was about 2 hours of dusk in the middle of the day. As there were no fresh vegetables, we had our daily ascorbic acid tablet to prevent 'scurvy', but certainly had nothing to complain about compared with the Forces in war zones and the horror of the bombing of so many UK towns, which we only heard about via the radio.

The most vivid memory of all, however, was that of the few weeks of the Aurora Borealis - the Northern Lights with its magnificent display and colour. In the evenings, we used to sit around the frozen lake crowded with expert skaters, in the centre of Reykjavik and enjoy the spectacle. The folds of the huge, vividly coloured curtain, seemingly hanging from the heavens above, wafting back and forth as if being blown by an unseen giant, appeared to hang so low as if to gently caress the skaters - a truly breathtaking sight.

By the time we returned to UK in July 1941 I was fortunate enough to have been promoted to Sergeant. We were stationed at Avebury in Wiltshire on the estate of the famous racehorse trainer, Fred Darling, where we saw some magnificent bloodstock including Classics winners. My rank entitled me to find private billeting in the village where Doris joined me for a couple of months.

The Unit was by now being rapidly re-equipped for service in the Middle East and the thought of the intense desert heat dismayed me. A few weeks before embarkation however, I was amazed and extremely relieved to be told I was being posted as an Instructor to Survey Training HQ at Wynnstay Hall near Ruabon in North Wales in the middle of beautiful countryside. I quickly sent out my heartfelt thanks to my 'angel guides' for their continued help. Being at Ruabon meant I was able to be home 12 hours after our son, Colin, was born on 23rd.February 1942 and enjoy a few days with Doris and our first-born. Life in the Sergeants' Mess at Wynnstay Hall was quite comfortable and I was privileged to be recommended for training as an officer in the Royal Army Ordnance Corps which, after 4 months rigorous training in the OCTU led to me being commissioned as a 2nd Lieutenant in July 1943.

After 6 months further training with the Motor Transport Spares Section at Chilwell, one of the large Army Ordnance Depots, I was posted to '14 Advanced Ordnance Depot' which had been mobilised to support the front line troops, in readiness for the Normandy landings in June 1944. The beach landing, a few days after D-Day, was rather unpleasant and scary, but the Unit remained intact to set up a Depot a few miles inland near the village of Audrieu, which I had the pleasure of revisiting a few years ago during our drive from Spain to Calais. It was our responsibility to keep the fighting units supplied with spares. This meant constant journeys to the coast and a drive out across the quarter mile of floating pontoons, on to the unloading area within the Mulberry Harbour, to collect the spares as the ships brought them in. The capitulation of Germany saw the Unit move forward to Glinde, near Hamburg, from where I was demobilised in March 1946.

So ended my '6 months Militia training' almost 7 years later and I returned to my job at British Titan Products in Billingham. I was back in 'civvie street' with a family of now three children and another one due within a few months. After years of responsibility in the Army, life as a lowly 'junior clerk', on little pay, proved to be rather frustrating and I needed to find a way of increasing our family income. A Fish and Chip shop partnership with my mother in December 1946 proved extremely helpful, topped up with a few extra pounds teaching Mathematics at some evening classes.

More important however, in the April, only 3 weeks after my 'demob', began the most amazing and joyful eight years of my 'social' life. During the regular Saturday night gathering at Syd and Gladys' house, Syd suggested that we sat for a 'Home Circle'. Little did we realise what wonders were in store for us and how privileged we were to be, that I would be writing a book about it fifty years later.

1945. The War's End. Back with the growing family

4

So what do we mean by ....

As this book, my story, concerns itself with psychic and spirit communication in its many various forms, through Mental and Physical Mediumship, I feel it makes sense to give you explanations at the outset of some of the main terms used to help you just in case you are unfamiliar with them.

SPIRIT WORLD - the Etheric World – the Soul World – the Mind World – all terms which are used to refer to what I always think of as 'The World Amongst Us'. When we leave our physical bodies, our Spirit, with its Etheric body, Mind and Soul, continues to live on, on a higher vibration, without the casing and impediment of the restrictive physical body. It takes up no physical space and can intermingle with the physical world without interfering, unless, and until we ask for contact. Personally I have always preferred the term 'The Spirit World' so that is what I shall use throughout this book.

Regarding its whereabouts - perhaps the nearest similarity or analogy I can offer you is the world of radio and television waves, which we cannot see or feel in our everyday surroundings. Yet they do surround us and are amongst us at all times, but only become 'real' or 'tangible' to us when we have a suitable receiver, like a radio or television set, to transform them into sound or vision which we can hear or see. The Spirit World is likewise around and amongst us on a higher vibration, but is also not evident to us through our five senses until we have the benefit of a human medium who can be used by our Spirit friends to transform the vibrations from the Spirit World into sound or vision. Spirit voices may be heard by mediums who have the gift of Clairaudience and hear 'mentally' or they may physically manifest sound through mediums who have developed the mediumship known as 'Direct Voice Control', like the voices we heard through the 'trumpet'.

Then, with ectoplasmic materializations, we not only hear their voices, we can see them standing amongst us in solid form. Both these types of extremely evidential phenomena and communication we were privileged to have throughout the years of our Home Circle, proving to us the reality of the Spirit World. It is not just a fanciful place, 'up in the heavens above', floating around in the clouds with wings and harps – not at all. Our trustworthy and reliable Spirit friends and relatives assure us it is absolutely real, permeating the space around us, intermingling with us, but never being intrusive in our lives.

PHENOMENA - the 'happenings' that occur through the gift of mediumship, whether 'Mental' or 'Physical'.

'Mental' phenomena includes the three main aspects of Clairvoyance (clear-seeing), Clairaudience (clear-hearing) and Clairsentience (clear-sensing), where the medium *alone* sees, hears or senses a contact from the Spirit World and is able to pass on messages to loved ones here. These types of phenomena are the ones usually demonstrated from platforms in churches or public halls and at one-to-one private sittings.

'Physical' phenomena differs distinctly from 'Mental', in that the phenomena is witnessed, that is seen, heard or sensed, by everyone in the room at that time. For physical phenomena to take place the medium is usually in a deep sleep-like state known as trance. There are many different types of 'physical' phenomena, including Vocal

Communication, Telekinesis, Apports, Spirit lights and Spirit writing. These five types of physical phenomena we were privileged to witness during the sittings of the Saturday Night Club and are detailed below.

Then, of course, there is Materialisation, where the Spirit people form solidly in the room with us. I have been extremely fortunate to meet, shake hands with, sometimes embrace and always able to converse with over 1,500 such solid, living, materialised Spirit people through the Physical mediumship of my mother, Minnie Harrison, in our Home Circle.

The majority of the Spirit people whom we, and our guests met, were relatives or friends whom we knew well during their earthly lives and recognised as precisely the same people, with the same characteristics, although temporarily inhabiting an ectoplasmic materialised body for as long as they could manage to stay. 'First-timers' could usually only manage a minute or two, whereas more experienced Spirits like Aunt Agg and Granny Lumsden would stay for up to 15 minutes.

From time to time we had Spirit visitors whom we had not known so closely, but who soon gave us clear evidence of their identity, which we were able to check. One particular visitor in this category was a well-known Spiritualist pioneer Alfred Kitson, whose visit I cover in a separate chapter.

After 18 months of sitting we were able to take a number of photographs in the red light, followed a year later, by some infra-red photographs, a selection of which are included in this book.

Vocal communication takes place in several ways: - through direct Spirit voices, where the medium is controlled by the Spirit person who speaks using the medium's vocal organs. (also known as 'trance control')

-through indirect or independent Spirit voices, where the voices come from mid-air through the use of a voice box built by the Spirit scientists

- by the means of a 'trumpet', which is simply, a lightweight cone-shaped megaphone made of a suitable malleable material like aluminium or plastic etc.

The most remarkable means of communication is when the ectoplasmic materialisation of the Spirit person stands before us and converses with us, face to face. This is indeed the most exciting and wonderful of all forms of phenomena.

Telekinesis – is the movement of an everyday physical or material object within, say, a room, without human contact.

In our Circle we regularly had a crinoline-lady shaped brass bell, weighing almost 2 pounds, which usually stood on the mantelpiece, (see p124, Tosher & Aunt Agg) ringing all round the room. Photograph frames were moved from the mantelpiece to other places in the room and there were similar movements of an ashtray, etc. I venture to suggest that Telekinesis occurs in our homes more often than we realise. How often have we put down a pen or pencil, or the car keys, in a specific place only to find they were not there when we return to collect them? Such movements may be frustrating at times but it is often only the Spirit children having some fun with you and we know we will come to no serious harm with them around.

These inoffensive happenings differ greatly from the destructive actions of poltergeists, who are generally sombre, forbidding, disorientated Spirits who are avid attention-seekers, using any unscrupulous means at their disposal. Should such unwelcome Spirits ever invade your privacy I strongly recommend you seek assistance from a reputable, highly recommended medium in your area, who should be able to persuade them to see the folly of their actions and guide them out of their self-imposed darkness to the higher Spirit regions of light. The celebrated Celtic medium from Glasgow, Albert Best, closely associated with Professor Archie Roy, gave long and extensive service, dealing successfully with such aggravating and sometimes frightening problems.

Apports, from left to right: -

Top row :-
Mr Roeder's Lyceum badge, bearing the picture of Andrew Jackson Davis, handed to me by the materialised form of Mr Roeder Sitting 89. (see Ch. 18)

Canadian 5 cent piece brought Sitting 5 (see Chapter 5)

One of the four red carnations handed to me by Aunt Agg on her first materialisation (Chapter 7)

Next row: -
Royal Artillery button apported on another of our 'Soldiers' nights

An old penny taken from my box at Lambeth Road and apported in the circle, 3 streets away. Identified by a sliver missing from the reverse in sitting 14. (Chapter 8)

The Lower Half of the photo: -
An orange feather brought by Sunrise to the circle's 1st anniversary sitting (Chapter 14)

A red silk Poppy brought during a sitting on one Remembrance Day.

Sprig of heather brought for 'Good Luck'. Just one of the hundreds of our floral apports.

A few of the Apports we received

Apports - (from the French 'apporter' – to bring) - are normal everyday items, which are moved from one place to another without human contact, through the solid barriers of walls and doors. Think perhaps of Apports as taking Telekinesis a step further along the path of Physical Phenomena. We had hundreds of apports throughout the years of our sittings, mainly flowers, but also coins and badges, as recorded in my weekly reports and I still treasure some of them in my memorabilia, which although priceless and irreplaceable, still accompany me on my talks.

The Spirit scientists told us they achieved this 'impossible' feat by either -

(a) de-materialising the item in question, which then having no material structure, could be brought through a solid wall and re-materialised again inside the room; or

(b) de-materialising part of the wall thereby creating a hole big enough for the item to be brought in – then re-materialising the aforesaid hole.

We were also given to understand that in the case of the Saturday Night Club they generally used the first method, which is akin to a similar procedure alluded to in the 'Star Trek' television series some years ago, when Captain Kirk commanded "Beam me up Scottie" and Scottie simply dematerialised the crew members, moved them and re-materialised them. I strongly believe the author of this series knew more than a little about physical phenomena – as with the author of the splendid film 'Ghost'.

You may also be interested to know that according to a report in 1998, scientists revealed that they have developed a 'Teleporter', which can transfer a particle of light from one part of their laboratory to another. "This is a great step forward," said Dr. Samuel Braunstein, an Australian lecturer at the University of Wales in Bangor, where the experiment took place. He has been working on the project with the Institute of Technology in Pasadena and added, "In the first experiment we teleported a particle of light over a distance of one metre, but now that the theory has been shown to work in practice, distance is no object. It works by decomposing something at one point and then reconstructing it at another location." The discovery will be used in the creation of new super-computers.

The Quantum Theory has been around for many years now and my attention was drawn to what Professor Paul Davies of Newcastle University said some years ago.

"Quantum Theory concerns the Alice in Wonderland realm inhabited by atoms and sub-atomic particles. On this microscopic scale the apparently solid material of such familiar objects as tables and chairs dissolves into an evanescent web of pulsing, shifting energy patterns. An electron can appear to be in two places at once or might suddenly dematerialise. They can perform startling tricks such as passing through 'impassable' barriers or bouncing off holes as well as objects. It simply does not have a well-defined position in space. Its behaviour is completely haphazard. The key feature of the Quantum domain is its unpredictability."

It has played a key role in the development of a host of inventions, from transistor radios to medical scanners and is being used to answer questions about the origin of the Universe. I cannot even pretend to understand the technicalities of such scientific matters but can only add that the Spirit scientists have been demonstrating such 'theories' for many years and I have a folder full of solid evidence. At least, it is good to know this world is beginning to catch up - at last.

Spirit lights - are produced by our Spirit friends, again without any human contact or earthly form of illumination. My notes show that we had our first four Spirit lights during Sitting 26 on 26th.October 1946. They were about one inch in diameter, lasted about two or three seconds and were clearly seen by all the sitters, in front of the fireplace. As the phenomena developed we had many more such lights, generally brighter than the first four. Often two or three would be seen at the same time and they would remain for up to ten seconds. This intriguing phase of phenomena was witnessed for a few months and then ceased until Sitting 80 on 22nd November 1947, when we were delighted to witness some exceedingly bright flashes of white light from behind the cabinet curtain, during the materialisation phenomena which we had been having for almost a year. There is nothing very significant about Spirit lights, but they are just another way of our friends showing their presence in a cheerful manner, and many people witness such lights in the peace and quietude of their darkened bedrooms.

Spirit writing - the same as with the Spirit lights, the writing done in our Circle was without any human contact.

I have to be specific about this, because there is another type of phenomena called 'Automatic Writing', where the medium holds the writing instrument and the hand is controlled by the Spirit people, who perform the writing process. The medium is completely unaware of the content of the writing and some mediums, in fact, do sit with their eyes closed, letting the hand do the writing 'automatically', beyond their personal control. Grace Rosher, the well known portrait painter who exhibited at the Royal Academy, was gifted with this 'Automatic Writing' type of mediumship and her book 'Beyond the Horizon' makes extremely interesting reading.

The writing in our Circle was completely without such human contact and took place in the darkness, during our sittings. During Sitting 6, I suggested that as another possible tangible means of showing our friends 'close presence' they could 'sign in' with the pencil on the sheet of paper resting, initially, on the hearth and then, later, on a table alongside me, but we had to wait until Sitting 17 for their first signatures. As another phase of our development, the signatures continued for a number

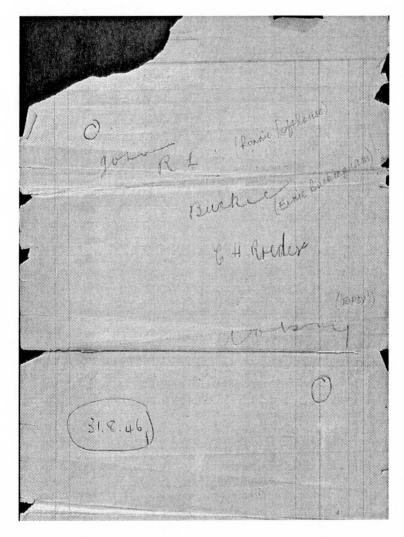

Spirit Writing: - A sheet of paper from Gladys' Accounts book showing the Spirit People who 'signed in' in sitting 18. The circles top and bottom was Sunrise's way of showing he was in control of the events. (I added the date and names in brackets after the sitting, to identify them.)

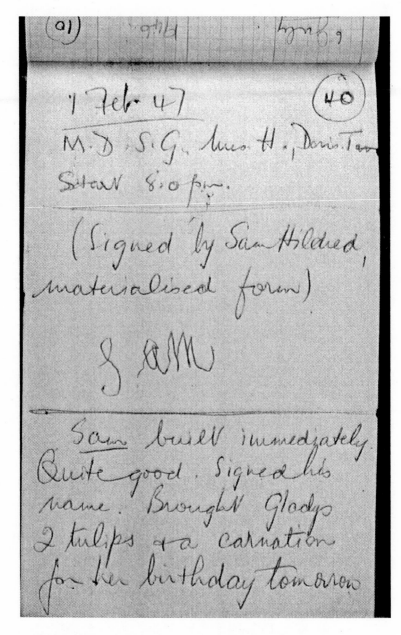

A photograph of the page of my notebook for Sitting 40 when Sam materialised in red light and signed his name in my book.

of weeks and I have the now rather faded sheets of paper, with the signatures still clearly readable, amongst my memorabilia. (see details in relevant chapters)

A distinctly different form of 'Spirit Writing' was witnessed during Sittings 38, 39 and 40, by which time we were having ectoplasmic materialised Spirit people standing in the room in a good red light. Aunt Agg came during Sitting 38 and I asked her would she like to sign her name in my notebook. I held my notebook in front of her, and she signed her name - Agnes.

During Sitting 39 Uncle Jack built and did likewise, followed, in Sitting 40, by Sam Hildred signing Sam. Here we have the rarity of three signatures made by materialised Spirit people, witnessed by everyone in the room, as permanent evidence of their actual presence amongst us. I remember reading of a similar experience in an account by Maurice Barbanell; a former Editor of 'Psychic News' and through whose trance mediumship was given the wise words of his Spirit guide Silver Birch. During a Physical Circle, with the medium Louisa Bolt, the materialised form of Sir Vincent Caillard wrote his signature on a piece of paper handed to him by Barbanell who considered this the greatest piece of evidence of life after death he had ever received. I am so thrilled to have not only one, but three such signatures of solid Spirit people, which are naturally still part of my notebook records - there for everyone to see.

ECTOPLASM - I make references to ectoplasm quite frequently throughout this book, but would like to introduce you to this unique substance that is produced by the chemists and scientists in the Spirit World. It is certainly *not* an unsubstantial, will o' the wisp type of matter referred to during sightings of ghosts or apparitions, which are often seen to walk through distant walls or just disappear into thin air. Whatever does make these 'visions' possible it certainly is not ectoplasm as we experienced it.

Ectoplasm is a tactile material which comes, originally, from the medium's body, in a gaseous form, through one or more orifices like the nostrils, ears or as in my mother's case, the mouth, as clearly seen on the infra red photographs we were privileged to take in December 1948. It must then return to the medium's body at the end of the physical phenomena and does not simply disappear into thin air, although sometimes, when inexperienced materialized Spirits make their departure, they seem to disappear into the ground, as though they were going through a trap door.

Let me assure you however that it only appears that way. There was certainly no trap door in the Shipman's carpeted lounge where we held our sittings. What is actually happening is that the Spirit person is unable to control the unfamiliar weight of physical material like ectoplasm and, being unable to support it, the ectoplasm is gradually taken back along the floor, by the scientists, into the cabinet where it is permanently attached to the medium. The Spirit people do not suffer, but find it very frustrating, and would often make such comments as they felt themselves going. The more experienced Spirits like Aunt Agg would simply walk back into the cabinet and close the curtain in readiness for the next person to materialize.

The Spirit scientists can create it in many different structural forms. One of the photographs shows it coming out of my mother's mouth, draped over her body in a diaphanous state, quite transparent – looking like very fine silk. The other shows it being used to 'operate' the trumpet, this time in a more solid rod-like form, which forms a shadow as seen in the photograph. Similar flexible rods are used to lift items in the room, such as the crinoline lady bell that they picked up and rang above our heads.

When it is used for the Spirit people to materialise, it is used to coat their etheric body, taking on a flesh-like format for the parts of the body, soft hair and beards when appropriate and rest flowing around them as robes of a very fine, soft drape, that we have felt on numerous occasions (see 'Granny Lumsden'). It is white in colour and seems to retain its whiteness in spite of the red light in the room. When we have shaken hands with our Spirit visitors, their hands are quite flesh-like and warm, as are their faces when we have kissed them. I cannot say that it became flesh-coloured because of the red light but it did look 'normal'. It truly is a unique, adaptable material produced by the Spirit scientists.

It is by no means a 'newly-discovered' material. It has been known by different names over the years. Professor Charles Richét coined the name Ectoplasm when he was President of the Society for Psychical Research in 1905. He derived it from Greek meaning 'Exteriorised substance'. Professor Thury referred to it as the *'Ectenic Force'*. Dr. W. J. Crawford carried out years of experiments with the Golligher Circle in Ireland and named it *'Cryptoplasm'*.

The great German authority Baron von Schrenk Notzing, who called it *'Teleplasma'*, sat with medium 'Eva C' between 1909 and 1913 to witness much phenomena and during that time he produced a chemical analysis as follows: "Colourless, slightly cloudy fluid with slightly alkaline reaction, traces of sputum, mucous membrane granules, potash, cell detritus, skin discs and minute particles of flesh," much the same as discovered by Dr. Dombrowski of the Polish Society for Psychical Research in 1916. Both the above analyses, which show traces of body matter, strongly support the fact that ectoplasm actually does come out of the body of the medium, as we certainly witnessed in the red light in our own Home Circle.

As long ago as 1874, Sir William Crookes FRS had numerous test séances over a long period with the young medium Florence Cook, through whose mediumship the materialised form of Katie King regularly appeared. During the final week of the tests Sir William successfully took 44 photographic plates of the materialised Katie, with some showing Florence Cook at the same time.

In May 1947, on two special occasions, Mr Brittain Jones, our surgeon member, was given permission to cut pieces of ectoplasm, about the size of a lady's handkerchief, from Aunt Agg's ectoplasmic gown, and during Sitting 52 Aunt Agg brought us an ectoplasmic feather. This was passed around the sitters before being placed in a jar on the mantelpiece - but I will cover these in greater detail during my reports of the actual sittings.

It is important at this point to emphasise the need for strict control of the sitters' actions during the sittings. Whenever physical phenomena is being produced by the use of ectoplasm, be it the movement of the trumpet or a fully materialised Spirit person in the room, the ectoplasm is always connected to the inside of the medium's body through whichever orifice is being used.

Any indiscreet, foolhardy or rash action like grabbing at or shining a white light on the ectoplasm can cause serious internal injuries to the medium, like the haemorrhaging, that occurred in the distressing case of Helen Duncan in 1956. The safety of the medium is of paramount importance at all times during a sitting. This is why the stringent 'vetting' of guests is a pre-requisite for attendance at a physical circle. In our case, my mother's life could have been at stake and we would have been responsible for such a tragic happening. The structure of ectoplasm may be seriously affected and even destroyed, by being confronted by white light. Its structure is unable to overcome the effects of the light – not dissimilar to the inability to develop or print photographs in white light. The chemical reactions cause the breakdown of the components in both cases.

So, ectoplasmic materializations can be dangerous to the medium, unless there is strict control in both worlds. It is imperative to follow the advice and instructions of the Spirit guides and helpers - in our case, Sunrise and Aunt Agg - then all will be well and trouble free.

On occasions, when the materialised forms stepped out from behind the 'cabinet curtain' hung across the corner of the room, we were very much aware of an unpleasant, pungent, acrid smell for just a few moments as they were leaving the cabinet. We could only assume that this was probably due to the ectoplasm emerging from my mother's body - but the odour soon faded.

Other people have told me they too have noticed such an odour in other materialisation Circles - but, like ourselves, it was never so unpleasant as to deter them from sitting. Such rare phenomena are far too precious to dismiss for such a minor discomfort.

I trust this will have given you a brief introduction to ectoplasm, without which substance, physical phenomena, especially 'materialisations', could never have been produced in any of the numerous well-attested Circles in those early days - like Helen Duncan, Alec Harris, Hunter Selkirk, George Sprigs, Jack Webber, to name just a handful, or even in our own Saturday Night Club of course. I have never seen any written explanation of how it is produced, although recently an explanation has been given at Stewart Alexander's Circle and this is included in that Chapter.

In response to our enquiries, all our Spirit friends could tell us was that they 'collected' the 'energy' within the room and 'mixed it' with some unique constituent inside the medium to produce and exude, through one or more orifices of the medium's body, the living, tactile substance we know as ectoplasm. They could not explain how they mixed the various constituents within the medium due to our lack of the necessary explanatory vocabulary.

As an additional point of interest, the presence or use of ectoplasm in today's physical phenomena Circles has diminished to such an extent as to become almost non-existent.

In such Circles, of which Ann and I have been privileged to be members, we have heard and felt, solid Spirit people walking round the room in the dark, without the use of ectoplasm. They told us they were very much aware of the dangers of ectoplasm and were now moving ahead, for the benefit of everyone concerned, by using the 'energy' in a different way. We can only confirm that they seem to be succeeding and they expect eventually to produce their own lighting to illuminate the materialisations as they walk around the room. We certainly look forward to those 'illuminating' phenomena.

MEDIUMS - people who have the 'ability' or 'gift' to link with the higher vibrations from individuals in the Spirit World and without whom this story would never have been possible. It is true that we are all born with this gift in some form or another – as often demonstrated by so many children talking to their 'imaginary' friends. Unfortunately it is so often suppressed by either the parents or the ridicule of their schoolmates, and established religious practices give them little support.

Those fortunate enough to have understanding parents, like my mother and myself, or strong enough to overcome the opposition and disapproval, may well develop their mediumship to be able to link with those higher vibrations, and bring to so many sad and bereaved people, the love, joy and comfort from their dear ones who have left the earth plane for a brighter, happier world of Spirit – now free of the restrictions of a physical body so often wracked with pain or disease.

As I have just said, these Spirit vibrations are permeating our environment at all times, in exactly the same way as television and radio waves. We would never be aware of any of them, however, without a suitable 'receiver'; a human medium for the spirit vibrations and a 'man-made mechanical medium' like a television or radio set for the latter.

I accept that this may be over-simplifying the situation but trust you 'get my drift'. It really is as natural and simple as that; subject to suitable conditions prevailing at the time, as the older 'wireless' buffs will recall with the old crystal wireless sets and the 'cat's whisker'. And who knows what the future holds? Serious experiments by scientific people are already under way to receive spirit vibrations without the 'known' presence of a human medium. Early results show promise of a 'mind-boggling' breakthrough in years to come.

CIRCLE - a group of people who sit together in a suitable room for the purpose of making contact with the Spirit World. The number of sitters can generally vary from three or four up to ten or twelve, but as close-knit harmony is an essential factor, it has been found that seven or eight are the ideal numbers. The group does not necessarily sit in a 'circle' as such, but sometimes in a horseshoe arrangement around a focal point. In our Home Circle we sat round the empty fireplace in the living room of our close friends, Sydney and Gladys Shipman, with my mother at one end and myself at the other. Another very good friend of ours in Hull has a spare room set aside in his house solely for their weekly sittings for physical phenomena - with excellent results –there we sit in a horseshoe around a corner where the medium sits and curtains can be drawn around him to concentrate the energy, but the type of room is not so important, so long as the ambience and atmosphere therein are conducive to the essential vibrations of harmony and true love.

I am sure that whenever you invite your friends and relatives to your home you meet them at the door with a smiling friendly welcome - full of joy and happiness - and the atmosphere to welcome your Spirit loved ones should be no less joyful - if anything, even more so. It is far more difficult for them to make contact than just walking up the path and knocking on the front door.

The prime purpose of our Home Circle was a regular weekly Saturday evening meeting between our friends from the Spirit World and us here on the earth. And always remember that laughter and joy are important basic ingredients of any successful Circle as I have always found throughout my many years of sittings.

For those who may be interested in forming their own Home Circles I would offer some important advice that we found so beneficial throughout the years of our sittings.

i) Be strictly disciplined with your sitting arrangements.

ii) Agree on a regular frequency of sitting (weekly, fortnightly or whatever), find a suitable night, place and time, and stick to them whenever possible.

iii) Do not let other leisure interests take precedence over your Circle arrangements. Your Spirit friends, with whom you are hoping to make contact, are entitled to such courtesy in the keeping an appointment: apart from the fact that they too have to make preparations – especially with physical phenomena.

iv) There must be complete sincerity and harmony of purpose amongst the sitters, each willing to give for the benefit of the whole. There is no place for egotists or self-seekers.

v) Give your room a friendly, cheerful and loving atmosphere, where your Spirit friends will be happy to accept your very warm invitation to make their presence felt in the manner they find most suitable at the time.

vi) The use of a brief opening prayer, welcoming our Spirit friends and asking for protection from mischievous Spirits, with a closing prayer of thanks, is something I cannot stress strongly enough. At the same time they give a definite format to the sitting - a beginning and an end.

You can never command or demand specific results – you are sitting to co-operate with them at all times and remember that every sitting is experimental. As you progress always be ready, as we were, to make any changes they may advise. Believe me they are as keen as you to improve the means of communication. From our first sitting we were advised to sit for trumpet voice phenomena which is assisted by complete darkness – so that is how we sat for this particular type of phenomena throughout the many years of our sittings – always in complete darkness, with tremendous success.

When, after only eight months, we were privileged to have ectoplasmic materialisation, our Spirit friends confirmed that we could use a red light to enable us to witness this remarkable and very rare type of phenomena. Starting with a small flash-lamp bulb and a battery in a wooden box, behind a piece of red glass, we progressed, as the phenomena developed, to larger brighter lights, with a dimmer switch connected to the mains electricity, to vary brightness, but these improvements were all on the advice of our Spirit helpers.

If you are sitting for physical phenomena, the energy is assisted by singing bright and cheerful songs particularly at the beginning. We used to sing nursery rhymes and popular songs which we all knew and could sing with gusto. We have been told that slow and ponderous hymns or tunes tend to have the wrong effect and deflate the vibrations. It doesn't matter whether you have good voices or not – it is the effort and joy you put into the singing that counts.

Recorded music can also be helpful – so use it if you feel the need, and join in when you can. Remember you are creating the atmosphere for a joyful get-together where laughter also plays an important part. Older readers will no doubt recall, before television, the fun-loving social evenings around the piano when we all had a good old sing-song and usually 'raised the roof with the energy created. Physical phenomena thrive on such energy.

Finally, do not exhaust yourselves by sitting or singing for too long, especially in the early days. We were advised to sit for no longer than an hour when we started, which was extended by our Spirit friends as and when they considered necessary. They will certainly let you know.

May your sincere and harmonious efforts be duly rewarded for the benefit of both worlds.

I hope these explanations will prove helpful and enable you to enjoy the stories that follow.

~~~~

My prayer.

In the long and silent watches
of the dark and dreary night,
My soul cries out in anguish
to the God of Love and Light.

Send down Thy Holy Angels in this my darkest hour,
That they may give me Light and Hope
and give my Soul the power
To rise above the sordidness of earthly cares and strife
That I may look to brighter things in that Eternal Life –

Where Love is crowned with happiness,
where all is fair and bright,
Where flowers bloom with sweet perfume
and where there is no night,

My Soul arises unafraid, my night of sorrow o'er,
Oh God of Love,
Thou leadest me towards that Heavenly shore.
My heart cries out with thanks to Thee
for all Thy loving care,
Into Thy hands I come –
Thou answerest now My Prayer.

Composed and dictated by Aunt Agg when she materialised on 21st July 1953, especially for Mr Brittain Jones)

5

'Who was who!'

So that you may relate to and recognise us as the story unfolds, here is a brief resumé of the members of, and frequent visitors to, our Home Circle. The Circle, started in 1946 quickly became known as 'The Saturday Night Club' or SNC and continued until my mother's passing in1958.

Home Circle Members

Minnie Rose Harrison, our medium,
by now 51; my mother had, from her teenage years, been both clairvoyant and clairaudient. She had already developed into a trance medium when we started the Home Circle. Her health was not good and she had had her first operation for cancer in 1940. (She passed over 1958.)

Thomas Henry Harrison, my father,
by now 56; known generally as 'Tosher', he had served on the Somme battlefield, been gassed and wounded before being demobilised in 1918 and now worked as a checker in the Railway goods yard. Not particularly mediumistic he provided much psychic energy. (He passed over in 1960.)

Thomas William Harrison, myself,
by now 27; newly returned from 7 years in the army throughout the war; some mediumistic awareness but more of a 'power giver'. I have a 'no nonsense' investigative outlook and cannot abide any semblance of pretension - especially where mediumship and psychic matters are concerned. Recorder of the circle.

The Saturday Night Club
Back row: Mr Brittain Jones; myself; my Dad; Sydney Shipman
Middle row: Mrs Hildred; my mother; my wife Doris.
Seated on the floor: Gladys Shipman

Doris Harrison, my wife,
by now 30; she was the second eldest in the large Hudson
family, a well-known Spiritualist family in Middlesbrough.
A State Registered nurse and Midwife, the devoted mother
of our six children, she was quite mediumistic, artistic and
very practical. A real family woman, never happier than
when surrounded by children.　　(She passed over 1976.)

Sydney and Gladys Shipman, our very good friends
and hosts for the sittings throughout the first six years in
their sitting room adjacent to their bakers and general
dealers shop in Middlesbrough.

Syd, by now 42; was a Master Baker and founder of
their Limited Company, He was raised in a Spiritualist
environment and has been very mediumistic throughout
his life; a practical man with a down to earth perceptive
outlook.

Gladys by now 30; became interested in Spiritualism
when she married Sydney in 1937. She was a good
business woman and a fellow director of their Company.

Florence Hildred, Gladys' widowed mother,
By now 56; she joined us soon after we started as her
husband Sam, who had passed over on Christmas Day
1945, started communicating regularly.
　　　　　　　　　(She passed over 1962.)

William Brittain Jones, FRCS,
by now 69; he was a highly respected senior surgeon in the
North East of England, Superintendent of Middlesbrough
General Hospital where Doris did her training, through
which contact we discovered his interest in psychic
matters. He joined us after we had been sitting for about
eight months. A small, enthusiastic and lively man with a
wealth of investigative experience in the medical field - so
lively indeed that he was known amongst the nursing staff

in the hospital as 'grasshopper', which he laughingly accepted.

Through his knowledge of infra-red photography and his contacts through the hospital, we were able to take infra-red photographs of the ectoplasmic phenomena, as shown in this book. He took the pulse of Aunt Agg's materialised body and in a later experiment cut off a piece of the ectoplasmic robe for analysis. (He passed over 1953.)

The eight of us made up the Saturday Night Club, here on the earth, but equally important of course, if not even more so, was the vast team of members working in the Spirit World. Apart from the special individuals who are listed below, we were told that for the ectoplasmic materialisations there was a team of about 20 chemists and scientists working behind the scenes to enable those Spirit visitors to build and meet us face to face.

Regular visitors from the Spirit World

Sunrise – *a North American Red Indian* - my mother's main Spirit guardian and guide who had been with her all her life on earth, and as we have heard him say to us in another Circle a few years ago, he is still working with her in the Spirit World. He was our Circle leader and doorkeeper in the Spirit World, protecting my mother from any interfering or malevolent Spirits who do not realise the serious damage they can cause by their spontaneous actions. He stepped in on a number of occasions over the years and always explained his reasons for so doing. His use of the English language at first was very limited, but he quickly learned and became a good communicator, especially through the trumpet - the lightweight megaphone, which stood on the floor in the centre of the Circle.

He would pick it up by means of an ectoplasmic rod emanating from my mother (see infra-red photograph) manipulate it all around the room, extremely rapidly, before bringing it to rest again, horizontally, in the centre of the Circle about three feet above the ground. From this position he would then speak to us and introduce, in turn, the Spirit people who were coming to communicate during that sitting. A completely dependable and faithful friend and a 'Chief' in every respect, he was always around in times of need.

Aunt Agg – *Mrs Agnes Abbott* – one of my mother's sisters, who had passed over in 1942. She had been a prominent medium at the Marylebone Spiritualist Association (now The S.A.G.B.) in London, from the mid 1930's until her sudden passing to the Spirit World, aged 57. She spoke and demonstrated in many of the well-known large halls in London, especially the Queen's Hall, and I have a faded copy of the 'Daily Mail' dated November 14th 1938 with a photograph of Aunt Agg, along with other well-known mediums, Nan Mackenzie, Mrs Barkel and Stella Hughes when they demonstrated at a special meeting in front of a packed house of 2,500 people - mainly war widows. Like my mother, she was an unassuming and homely woman who always found time to help those in need; a kind person who would never speak ill of anyone, but strong enough to speak out when the need was there.

She was one of the mediums who sat for the Church of England's investigation into Spiritualism in 1937, the report of which remained unpublished until around 1948 when someone leaked it to A. W. Austen at the Psychic Press.

Arthur Findlay also had trance sittings with her at the MSA and an account of one of the sittings, at which his mother communicated, is recorded in his book 'Looking Back' and in later editions of 'On The Edge of the Etheric'.

Aunt Agg became a major link between the two worlds, materialising every week and generally being the last to come to close the sitting.

Granny Lumsden – Doris's maternal grandmother, who passed over in 1930 in her mid-seventies; another person who spent much of her time looking after the needs of others when she lived in Lonsdale Street in Middlesbrough. She was seldom seen without her large shawl draped around her shoulders (just like the ectoplasmic shawl seen in the photograph), running errands for the elderly and housebound.

She was a very warm and cheerful personality who always materialised with a spontaneous chuckle and cheery word for all the sitters, especially any guests. I have written a separate chapter to tell you more about Granny's antics. There was never a dull moment when she was around.

Sam Hildred - Gladys Shipman's father

He passed suddenly at Christmas 1945. He soon became a first class communicator through the trumpet. A most likeable and friendly man, he obviously enjoyed his weekly chat with his wife and daughter. He spoke in a very clear voice and in his own unmistakable manner, definitely recognised by his wife, daughter and son-in-law Sydney, week after week. A very interesting point here is that when he was on the earth plane he always called Gladys - *'Gladdy'*, which no one else did, and when he spoke to her through the trumpet it was still always *'Gladdy'*! Sam was still the same Sam and Dad. We do not suddenly change!

Uncle Jack - John Bessant - one of mother's brothers

He passed over in 1927. Uncle Jack was also a trance medium and gave me my first experience of seeing someone in trance when I was 3 or 4. He was killed in a works accident when he was 40.

Mona Hildred - Gladys' sister - passed over 1933,
                                        aged 12 years

Douglas Hildred - Gladys' brother - passed over 1928,
aged 5 days
Ivy Hudson - one of Doris's sisters - passed over 1922,
aged 1 year

Frequent guest sitters
Mam and Dad (Annie and Charles) Hudson - Doris's parents

Mrs Shipman - Sydney's mother

Jim Mckenzie - Took the first two photographs of our
  Spirit visitors - Aunt Agg and Granny Lumsden;
  - recorded our Christmas Party sitting in 1954.

~~~~

When I am gone

No funeral gloom, my dears, when I am gone;
Corpse-gazing, tears, black raiment, graveyard grimness;
Think of me as withdrawn into the dimness, -
Yours still – you mine; remember all the best
Of our past moments – and forget the rest.

Cremate my body then my dears, when I am gone;
Think of my soul in realms supernal,
Returning oft to earth from the Eternal;
Yours still – you mine; united still in love
Till God shall call you too, my dears – above.

<div align="right">M.R.H.</div>

6

'S N C' - The First Three Months

Saturday evenings were sacrosanct, an evening for socialising; for us, a chance to spend the evening with Sydney and Gladys Shipman in their very friendly home adjacent to their bakery and general dealer's shop in Burlam Road. Mam, Dad and Doris had enjoyed their visits every Saturday during most of the War years, and when I was on leave from the Army I joined them; plus, whenever I was stationed in the UK, I made every effort to get to a call box and ring Syd and Gladys to talk to Doris and Mam.

So, quite unknowingly, the six of us had made a very strong bond, which proved so important when the war ended and I was demobilised in March 1946. Five of us had been brought up in Spiritualism and Gladys, a Methodist, was very interested. My mother, now just 51 and as I have already said a 'natural' medium, had developed into a good 'deep trance control' medium like one of her elder sisters Agnes - known to us as Aunt Agg - who had passed over in 1942.

Aunt Agg was able to control my mother remarkably smoothly, and within a minute or two would be talking to us, although my mother was unaware of what was happening and afterwards remembered nothing of Aunt Agg's visit. She simply 'went to sleep' in the knowledge that she would be protected by the empathy between them. It was a unique, loving relationship, which continued throughout her life, and in the comfort of our own home, sitting around the fireplace, we were often the delighted recipients of such treasured moments.

Our Saturday evenings were always enjoyable, with musical duets by Sydney on his violin and Gladys, an accomplished pianist. Unknown to us however there was a far more important purpose to that weekly get-together. One Saturday, about three weeks after I had been demobbed, Sydney suggested we had a 'Home Circle'. We were all in enthusiastic agreement, and arranged to start it the following week, not knowing what results we would have.

Our expectations were, at best, to make contact with our Spirit friends through the trance mediumship of my mother, something very special, which could not just be 'turned on' like a tap. Little did we know what a remarkable future lay ahead for us. Some months later Aunt Agg told us that our rapid progress was due, in no small measure, to the 'energy bank', which had been built up in Sydney and Gladys' room during those five years of meeting there during the war.

Thus, on 6th April 1946 our unique 'Saturday Night Club' was born. It was dedicated to a weekly meeting between us and our friends in Spirit and that was the way it remained throughout our years of sitting - at the express desire of our Spirit helpers and guides.

As the years progressed they were happy to agree to suggested changes or experiments, the use of a red light, taking photographs, infrared photography etc. It was, however, never to become a scientific research Circle with 'professional' researchers, who are never convinced, and would have put my mother through the discomfort and indignity of taping her mouth and roping her to the chair as they had with so many others. My mother would arrive at Sydney and Gladys' home a short while before the start of our sitting and just sit chatting on the dining chair which was hers for the evening. We were all aware of her sincerity to sit for the benefit of our Spirit friends and we all *knew* the phenomena were absolutely genuine. This was confirmed by all our guests, particularly Roy Dixon Smith and Ernest Thompson (Editor of 'Two Worlds' journal).

Without the dedication of our Spirit helpers, no way could my mother have produced such masses of ectoplasm, formed it into solid 'living' recognisable Spirit people walking around the room in good red light, whilst she was sitting in her chair in deep trance, in full view of everyone there. Such was the simple purpose of our weekly sitting - to bring together people from both worlds.

I invite you to become a guest sitter and enjoy our remarkable experiences.

To ensure that the facts about the sittings are correct I have alongside me the notes that I made for the first two years immediately after each sitting, whilst enjoying Gladys' supper. I realise now I should have made more copious notes for a longer period, but at that time we did not appreciate the future significance of our sittings. As far as we were concerned it was a simple, very private Home Circle helping the guest sitters we were able to invite. It was all so natural and we just thought it would go on, and on, which it did for about eight years, before Mam's cancer finally took its toll and left a massive gap in our lives.

However I still have those basic facts and very clear, joyful memories, from which extracts will be presented to you throughout this book. If you can enjoy reading them even one tenth as much as we and our guests enjoyed experiencing them, my writing will not have been wasted. And hopefully your minds will have been expanded concerning the Truth of Life after Death.

In an earlier chapter I have explained about the conduct of Circles in general so now you are ready for the phenomena, which occurred during our sittings.

Saturday 6th April 1946. 8.30 pm.
Sitters – Mam, Dad, Syd, Gladys, Doris, Tom. (we were the weekly 'regulars', and so from now on I will only enter visitors' names at the beginning of a sitting. Later, Mrs Hildred and Mr Jones also became regulars).

Tonight the opening prayer was given by Sydney but from our third sitting onwards we opened by saying, in unison, a prayer called 'Invocation to Angels' which we knew from our years attending the Lyceum - the educational Sunday school of the Spiritualists National Union.

Not knowing exactly what phenomena or messages we might receive, if any, you may be surprised to hear that we actually sat round the dining table with the letters of the alphabet spread round and an up-turned wine glass in the centre,* in the hope that we would get some guidance concerning the future overall conduct of our sittings. Three or four of us, excluding my mother, placed a finger lightly on the glass, which soon began to move round and round quite fast. No letters were indicated and within a few minutes the glass was rapidly moved off the table altogether - being caught by one of the sitters.

A few minutes later we were thrilled to hear Aunt Agg, for the first time for many months, speaking through my mother who was now in deep trance. She assured us there was no need for us to use such methods, and after a general chat advised us, unexpectedly, to sit with a trumpet (a lightweight megaphone) - something we would have never even thought about. Such phenomena is extremely rare and we had no idea that my mother had that potential in the same way as Aunt Agg, who had been an excellent trumpet medium in her own Home Circle, in London.

As soon as Aunt Agg finished speaking, her main guide, a North American Indian called Running Water, who still works with her in the Spirit World, took over and spoke to us; another very exciting moment. He confirmed his medium's advice and assured us we would get as good results as she did! It was very difficult at that time for us to comprehend such promises when the best we had ever expected was regular trance mediumship. Within a few minutes of Running Water leaving us, my mother came out of her trance and we closed the sitting with a prayer of thanks.

When we told Mam what had occurred, she found it hard to believe, and we were all very excited at the future possibilities. Syd agreed to make a trumpet ready for the next sitting which we were all eagerly anticipating including my mother. What an unexpected, exciting start! The 'buzz' in that room was quite electric.

* Footnote re Ouija boards etc.

From what we have been told by our Spirit helpers, the wine glass, the 'ouija' board or typtology (table tilting) are quite credible and acceptable methods of 'mediumship' so long as the sitters have the correct attitude and ask for protection from the Spirit people helping them. Problems generally arise when the sitters, often very energetic teenagers, decide to sit and 'let's have some fun'. The doors are then open to all kinds of mischievous Spirits (and there are always plenty around) often bent on causing mayhem, which then gives these methods a very bad name .

Over the past 10 years, when no well-developed medium was available, Ann and I have successfully used these methods to receive excellent messages and guidance, without any problems. Over the years I have known many reputable people who have successfully done likewise. The choice is yours of course, but always have a happy, positive and well-founded outlook to attract the right kind of genuine and harmonious Spirit people whose messages you may well find helpful, encouraging and supportive. Above all, they could offer you verifiable evidence, perhaps unknown to you, of the continuity of Life after Death - the validated knowledge of which can 'transform your life' - as so many others have previously discovered.

From hereon, for ease of reference, I have given the Sittings sequential numbers.

13th April. 8.30 pm. (1)

Gladys' mother Mrs Hildred joined us tonight. Her husband Sam had passed over quite suddenly during the previous Christmas holidays.

Syd had made a metal trumpet, which we placed on the floor in front of the fireplace, around which we sat in a semi-circle. We had no Spirit communication through my mother and as we were sitting in darkness - as advised the previous week - we could not tell whether the trumpet had moved at all. After about half an hour I mentally asked that they might knock over the trumpet to signify time to close and after about 15 minutes we all heard it fall over. When we switched on the light after closure we checked that none of us had stretched a leg and actually kicked the trumpet. Whether it was in response to my request mattered not - it had been moved without physical contact. As I say in my notes - "A good start".

Saturday 20ʰ April,

We had no sitting this week, because about 8.15 pm as we were preparing to sit, a knock on the door heralded the unexpected arrival of two of Gladys' cousins who were passing through Middlesbrough and decided to make a surprise call. It certainly took us all by surprise and the word was quickly spread around not to visit Sydney and Gladys' on a Saturday evening as they had some regular visitors - little did they know who! However there was a very interesting happening that evening.

Sydney had an electric clock on the mantelpiece that he tended regularly - his special interest is horology and he repaired watches and clocks for friends. This clock never stopped unless he was working on it, but much later during this particular evening someone noticed it had stopped *at exactly 8.30 pm* - the time we would have been starting. Coincidence? We think not.

We were sure that our Spirit friends were indicating they were still there irrespective of the visitors. We had no more unexpected visitors from that day onwards. As far as I know the clock has never unexpectedly stopped since, and is still working on their mantelpiece at Robin Hood's Bay in North Yorkshire.

27ᵗʰ April 8.30 pm. (2)

My mother was controlled by Sunrise who again promised us good results. He also advised us on the position of the sitters thus:

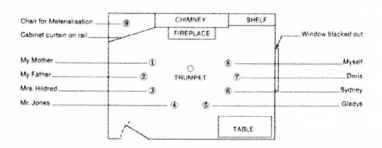

(The room was an ordinary furnished living room about 12 feet square so you can imagine there was very little space between the 8 chairs and I have tried to portray the fireplace etc. to scale.)

We heard knocking on the floor, which we were told was the Spirit children and we were told the trumpet had moved although we could not see it.

Note: We started 15 minutes earlier from tonight until 6ᵗʰ July; from then we started at 8pm until December 1947; when, because the sittings were getting longer, we started at 7.30pm.

4ᵗʰ May 8.15pm. (3)

The trumpet tapped in time with our singing towards the end of the sitting at 9.15 pm.

Tonight we had our FIRST APPORT!!! It was a small piece of white blossom, like flowering cherry, which Sydney found under the trumpet when he lifted it, after the sitting had closed. We checked with all the sitters that they had nothing like it on their persons and that Gladys had no such blossom in the house. Sydney then said, prophetically, as it turned out, 'This must be our *first* apport' - which assumed we would get more in the future. How right he was - we had hundreds of apports over the years, mostly flowers of various kinds, but other items which I shall record as we progress. Although the blossom had no scent, at the same time as Sydney lifted the trumpet the room was filled with a delightful overwhelming scent of pinks for just a few minutes. As my notes record - 'Everyone very excited'.

11ᵗʰ May. (4)

We realised that the blackout of the window was not as good as it should be but we still had our sitting with good results. Again the trumpet tapped on the floor keeping time with our singing. When the light was switched on, at the close of the sitting, we noticed that a metal ashtray had been moved from the mantelpiece on to a cabinet alongside the fireplace some three feet away (Telekinesis phenomena). We immediately compared weights with the trumpet - the ashtray weighed one and a half ounces and the trumpet three and a half ounces, so with an improved blackout, which Sydney did arrange, we had high expectations for more movement from the trumpet next week. No flower apport this week, but when Sydney went upstairs after the sitting he found a sprig of lilac in his bedroom. No perfume.

18ᵗʰ May (5)

The complete blackout gave excellent results. There was a great feeling of power with the men feeling cold and the women feeling hot! At the end of our third song we heard something drop on to the fireplace, which we found to be a Canadian 5 cent coin dated 1889. (a separate chapter about this coin later). The trumpet tapped Dad, Mam and Gladys on their knees - then we heard, very faintly, a voice speaking through the raised trumpet, saying "I am trying; I am trying, that's all for now." We learned later that the voice belonged to Aunt Agg, who, because of her previous experience was generally the first to try something new. Wonderful - we had had a trumpet voice during only our fifth sitting - remarkable. Then, when the light went on, there was a sprig of Lily of the Valley at my feet (another apport) with a slight scent of pinks pervading the room again. My report says - "Excellent sitting", and so it was!

25th May (6)

This week I placed a sheet of paper and pencil on the hearth alongside me and invited our Spirit friends to leave us a message if possible. When the light went on there was no sign of any movement. We had to wait until Sitting 17 for the first signatures.

Prompt rappings with the trumpet from the first song. The trumpet came round the circle and tapped everyone except Doris who was expecting our fourth child very soon. Aunt Agg then conversed quite clearly for about five minutes and advised us about improvements to the trumpet - larger bell end to stop resonance. Mam, who had been in light trance control, said later she had felt queer in her throat when Aunt Agg was speaking. When the light went on all the items on the mantelpiece had been switched around (more telekinesis) and in the narrow end of the trumpet, as it stood on the floor was a tulip (another apport) using the trumpet like a vase. "Excellent progress" says my report.

1st June (7)

By now we had improved the trumpets and actually had four in total - one metal, one plastic, one cardboard and one in plywood that Sydney made in a pyramidal style. (This plywood trumpet proved very useful in August when we painted the lower half of one side with white paint and it was used by our Spirit friends as a plaque to show us ectoplasmic hands)

Our thinking was that our friends would be able to select which they found most suitable. Within a short period of starting this week we were amazed to hear that all four trumpets were being used at the same time, which, you will appreciate, took a tremendous amount of energy. Before we started I wrote a question on the paper on the hearth 'Who is the apport medium?' and the answer was soon forthcoming from Aunt Agg when she spoke through one of the trumpets...."Collective power." Her voice was much stronger and clearer. Uncle Jack then controlled the wooden trumpet which was quite weighty, and joined in singing with one of our songs after Aunt Agg had finished. He then spoke to us, very clearly, and told us to keep on telling his widow, Aunt Harriet who was not sure about such matters. My father then said he wasn't sure it was Jack, and a quick response came through the trumpet... "Of course it's Jack, you softy" (one of his favourite expressions). Dad immediately apologised to which Jack replied "I should think so!" A very interesting brief altercation between the two worlds!

When the light went on at the end of the sitting we saw that all the items on the mantelpiece had been switched around again, and they had laid a beautiful Pyrethrum across the narrow end of the wooden trumpet - very delicately balanced.

As my notes recorded, 'Continued progress - excellent results'.

We never found out which of our four trumpets they preferred because, for holiday reasons, we had no sittings for two weeks until 22nd June, by which time we had received Aunt Agg's light weight aluminium trumpet from her own Home Circle in the 1930's! I remembered that her daughter Gwen in London had kept her mother's trumpet as a souvenir of her wonderful mediumship. A few weeks after we had started sitting I had written to Gwen and told her of our exciting news. Would it be possible, I asked her, to borrow Aunt Agg's trumpet for a few weeks to help us along. Her response was quick and generous. We could certainly have the trumpet for as long as we wanted and she knew her mother would be very happy with her decision. She immediately posted it to us and we used it for the first time on Saturday 22nd June.

This trumpet is still in my possession and apart from use in our Home Circle in Middlesbrough, it has 'seen service' in at least three other physical Circles in the UK. It is 21 inches long with a 3.5" diameter at the bell end, is now over 70 years old, well battered and dented, and is a very prized and cherished part of my memorabilia, which accompanies me on all my talks. Members of the audiences just love to come up after the talks to hold it and feel the energy still emanating from it. The bell end was getting so misshaped after a few weeks of beating time to the music by knocking it on the floor in 1946, that Sydney riveted a band of thicker aluminium round it - which remains there to this day. It had no adverse effect on the phenomena.

22nd June (8)

First sitting with Aunt Agg's trumpet, which had three small spots of luminous paint on the bell end making it clearly visible in the blacked-out room. It was fascinating and exciting to watch its rapid movements around the room, darting up to the ceiling, pirouetting around the room, gently touching some of the sitters on their knees - all in complete darkness, without knocking into lampshades or other pieces of furniture; quite remarkable! We were also given some identifying movements for three of our Spirit friends - Sunrise made the sign of a circle, indicating the sun; Aunt Agg simply moved it up and down in short vertical strokes, and Sam knocked it hard on the floor — 'Aye-tiddly-aye-tie, tie-tie.' (hope you can understand what I am trying to express). At future sittings we had other different signals for many other new Spirit members. A real happy family atmosphere!

Aunt Agg spoke to us through the trumpet and then Sunrise cleared the way for Sam Hildred who spoke very forcefully but could not stay long. Ivy Hudson, Doris's sister who had passed as a baby many years ago, spoke to

Doris, quite clearly. Uncle Jack then joined in the singing again and picked up Gladys' crinoline lady brass bell from the mantelpiece, weighing almost two pounds, and rang it vigorously for a few seconds. No apport this week but during the following week Sydney could not find his penknife, which he used every day. He found it on the Thursday under the trumpet, which during the week stood in the corner of the sitting room where we held our Circle! In response to our request, Sunrise told us they would let us know when we could invite guest sitters - which we were keen to do. We wanted to share these wonderful experiences. Excellent progress again.

After a number of sittings with Aunt Agg's trumpet, Gladys, commented during the sitting, that Sunrise always scribed his circle in the same direction - maybe clockwise. Immediately she had spoken the trumpet stopped dead, then rapidly scribed in the opposite direction - anti-clockwise. Sunrise had obviously heard the comment and reacted! From that evening onwards he always scribed it in both directions - the same as he does in another Circle of which Ann and I were weekly members for some years and now have the pleasure and privilege to visit whenever we are in UK.

Around this period, before we received Aunt Agg's trumpet, we were trying to obtain some luminous paint to dab on the trumpets, but without success - not surprising so soon after the end of the war. However I remembered an old watch I used to have with luminous spots on a black face and thought this would be useful. During the week, I searched the drawers at home but could not find it. Mam did likewise at their house with similar results. But it was not so difficult for our Spirit friends.

29th June (9)

This week we thought it might be helpful to put a luminous rabbit toy on the mantelpiece, but soon realised we were wrong. It was far too distracting and we removed it after five minutes. The trumpet movements were very good and 12 of our Spirit friends gave their signs. Sunrise spoke very clearly and told us there was great power and everyone on their side was very pleased. He then asked us to start at 8 pm and finish at 9 pm – which we did from the next week. Mona Hildred, Gladys' sister who had passed over when she was 12, tried to speak but could only laugh. Sunrise told us this, and that he was now the new leader from their side as he could use the trumpet better than Aunt Agg.

He told us that the medallion, found under Gladys' settee, had been brought by Ivy Hudson from her mother's house in Ayresome Park Road, about half a mile away - and she had brought another apport which we would see at the end of the sitting. He also told us that Sydney's knife had been moved by Sam Hildred (telekinesis). Then Dad's mother spoke, very faintly but quite clearly.

Uncle Jack followed, very clearly, and advised on treatment of Aunt Harriet's painful leg, particularly "to write to that fellow Edwards"; a reference to the renowned healer Harry Edwards. I told Aunt Harriet the next day but, because of her lack of belief, I don't know whether she ever did write. Sunrise told us a new Spirit member had joined us that night - Ernie Buckingham, a Lyceum friend of ours, who had passed over through a stroke in his early twenties. My notes show that we had 35 minutes of conversation during this sitting - wonderful progress!

When the light went on there were, not only four sprigs of ivy from Ivy, in return for the flowers her Mam had sent for her, but there on top of the clock on the mantelpiece was my old watch! They had found it from somewhere and brought it to the Circle - a rather special apport! During the following week I removed the luminous face, cut it into four pieces and Sydney stuck them on the four sides of the wooden trumpet so now we had two trumpets with luminosity.

The following week, during Sitting 10, I put what was left of my watch back on top of the clock and after thanking them for bringing it, simply said they could take it back - wherever that was. At the end of the sitting the watch had disappeared. It was later found in the drawer of the cabinet in the room with some of the other apports - another example of telekinesis coupled, this time, with 'dematerialisation' to put it in the drawer without the drawer being physically opened - unless the Spirit folks actually opened the drawer themselves. We never asked, as we were just so thrilled that we had experienced so much physical phenomena so quickly.

So ended the remarkable first three months of our sittings, and the phenomena had been far beyond our hopes or expectations when we started. But it proved to be only the beginning of even more wonderful phenomena to come in the months and years ahead. The unbelievability of it all; the 'boggle factor' as I call it; frequently impressed itself on our minds - particularly when we were privileged to have materialised ectoplasmic Spirit people joining us in the middle of our Circle - but I am jumping ahead a little.

7

The Canadian five-cent coin, dated 1889

It was during Sitting 5 on Saturday 18th May 1946 that we had received our second Apport - a silver coloured Canadian five-cent coin dated 1889, as I had recorded in my notebook at the end of the sitting. It was only six weeks since we had started sitting in our Home Circle so we were thrilled to have been so privileged in such a short time. Our first apport, the piece of white cherry blossom, during our third sitting, had soon decayed, as any piece of blossom would do naturally.

But here we had a solid metal apport, which we would be able to keep. Where it had come from we never discovered, unlike some of our later apports, but we know that our Spirit friends never bring such articles from places where they would cause any kind of upset, annoyance or frustration to the previous owners. They are never items of great material value - which was certainly the case in our experience.

The coin was kept amongst our other memorabilia, which, when I was giving my talks in later years from 1967 onwards, I carried with me for the audiences to inspect. Such smaller apports were kept for safety in plastic envelopes secured in a hard-backed folder. Before leaving home for each talk, I would check all my equipment including the various very precious apports. During one such check, in March 1990, I noticed that the five-cent coin was missing and that there was a hole in the bottom corner of its envelope. Naturally I was rather upset; I checked through all my carrying bags, but all to no avail - the coin must have fallen out somewhere. Still, there was nothing I could do about it and continued with my talks travelling countrywide.

After Doris had passed over in 1976 I remarried and so at this time I was living near High Wycombe in Buckinghamshire with my second wife, who, in 1991, needed a hip replacement operation.

We each had a car but for some weeks after the operation she was unable to drive. As she found her car door more accessible, we put a cushion on the passenger seat and I did the driving - leaving my car in the garage. One of my daughters, Joyce, who lives in Somerset, had to visit Slough hospital for regular examinations after an operation. The arrangement was that Joyce would travel by coach to Slough, only 10 miles from our house, and I would collect her to take her to the hospital. On this particular occasion in 1991 I used my wife's car, complete with cushion on the passenger seat, to collect Joyce from the hospital as she had had a lift with a friend to London that morning. I parked in the hospital car park and Joyce duly arrived after her examination.

As I opened the passenger door I told her to remove the cushion if she didn't want it, and walked round to the driver's side expecting her to be in her seat by the time I had walked round. Instead she was still standing outside the car holding something small in her hand. She had put the cushion on the back seat and as she went to sit down had noticed a small coin on the seat, which must have been under the cushion. As she held it up she asked me what it was and handed it to me.

I was absolutely amazed to find it was a Canadian five-cent coin, the date was 1889 and it looked exactly the same as the one I had lost! Admittedly I had no identification marks on the apported coin but just *knew* that our Spirit friends had brought it back from wherever it had been. So it had been *apported for a second time* some 45 years later and re-materialised under the cushion in the dark. Wonderful!

I must emphasise that at no time had I ever used my wife's car when travelling to give a talk, so at no time could the coin have fallen out into her car, especially on the passenger seat. It would be a most remarkable coincidence for an identical coin to just happen to be on the car seat that day. We don't know whether it had been under the cushion for some days previously, although I very much doubt it, but even so, it had certainly been apported from somewhere - another piece of splendid evidence that under the right conditions, apports can occur anywhere and at anytime.

Needless to say it is still amongst my treasured memorabilia, safe and secure in a new, stronger plastic envelope and still travels with me on my talks.

8

'S N C' - July to November 1946

During the next five months our sittings evolved into a regular format with 'trumpet signs' from our regular Spirit visitors, many apports and greatly improved direct voices through the trumpet. To save space and avoid boring you, I will simply tell you about any significant happenings, and in some cases perhaps, just give you a copy of the notes from my notebooks.

For the next 10 sittings we were joined by Terry Abbott, Aunt Agg's youngest son, who was a semi-professional photographer. In February 1948 he would take the last batch of photographs for the circle.

By now you, like us, are probably wondering where the apported flowers came from; remember apports are physical objects which are moved from one place to another without any earthly human contact, even, as in our case, into a room with the door and window locked.

Over the years we had well over a hundred. In the early days when we were getting perhaps just one or two flowers, Aunt Agg told us they got them from the neighbours' front gardens or nearby allotments. The row of houses adjoining the shop had small front gardens so we used to walk along and have a look to see if to there were similar flowers there - and there usually were. When it was wet weather the apported flowers were wet, which indicated they had been obtained from an outside source that evening.

In later sittings we began to receive small bouquets of various flowers, which would be laid on the hearth and had obviously not been taken from an outside garden. Aunt Agg's reply, given with her inimitable chuckle, was quite unexpected. Just along the road from the Shipman's shop was a small florist's shop, which we often used. She explained that all the flowers were put into a shed behind the shop (no temperature controlled rooms in those days) and they would be there until Monday morning, by which time many would have died. So, as it was now Saturday evening and some were already wilting - they were 'liberating' them before it was too late - and the florist was none the worse off financially.

We felt it sounded very logical and were happy to continue receiving our lovely apports, which were often brought to us to be passed on to someone in need of support, or for a birthday memory, with a few joyful words from a loved one in the Spirit World.

13ᵗʰ July (11)

A lot of power. Apported flowers brought at once - double pyrethrum for Doris. For Mrs H. there was a piece of Southernwood for her own garden. Sam Hildred spoke through the trumpet within a few minutes, even before Sunrise, who usually came first, speaking very clearly to tell her he had brought it for her - another special apport. Unbeknown to the rest of us Mrs Hildred had visited her sister just before coming to sit. As they were walking round her garden Mrs H. saw some Southernwood which has a beautiful scent and said to her sister that she would like a cutting sometime for her own garden. This conversation had taken place less than two hours before we met, yet when we put on the light at the end of sitting there it was waiting for her. Mona Hildred, who passed over as a 12 year old in 1933, then spoke to her mother and said "Big girl now, Mam."

Aunt Agg spoke to Terry and told him she had brought his cufflinks from his house to show she was often close to him. The cufflinks were on the hearth at the end of the sitting. Our usual sittings lasted about an hour when

Sunrise told us to close, but tonight the trumpet fell to the floor before he had told us to close and we realised something was wrong. We immediately closed and found the circle had lasted only 50 minutes.

The following week Sunrise apologised but explained that he had had to close so abruptly because an unknown Spirit onlooker had suddenly tried to control the trumpet, which could have caused problems for my mother, but thanks to Sunrise she was unaffected. Apparently the onlooker had been a suicide case who was then helped by our Spirit friends to understand where he was and how he could progress in the Spirit World.

This highlighted the need for, and the value of, a strong Leader in the Spirit World, such as Sunrise, particularly with physical phenomena. We were told that there are many Spirit onlookers at each sitting who are greatly helped in their search for progress, and are attracted by the beacon of light (spiritual/psychic energy) that emanates from Circles like ours. So it is good to know we help so many people who are in need, and on only three occasions in the six or seven years of sittings was Sunrise's similar intervention necessary.

20th July (12)

Flowers apported included a double marigold, a red-tinted carnation and a yellow carnation for Aunt Agg's daughter, Madge, whose birthday was the next day. We were delighted to receive the flower, which we took to her on the Sunday.

Sam's photograph was moved on the mantelpiece and we heard clickings and tappings, which sounded like human fingernails. Sunrise told us they were experimenting with different phenomena and Mam felt a hand touch her (confirmed by Sunrise).

Mrs Nellist (known as 'Ma') was our new Spirit member and she was powerful enough not only to pick up the trumpet, but to move the heavy brass 'crinoline lady' bell, from the mantelpiece into the mouth of the trumpet, and ring it loudly from inside the trumpet. Exceptional energy needed to do that on her first visit.

Sunrise then told us we could have our first guest sitters but they must be partners, so that the energy they brought would be more easily blended than two people who were strangers to each other. We had no difficulty in deciding that it should be Doris's parents, Annie and Charles Hudson, who were long-standing members of Middlesbrough Spiritualist Church.

27th July (13)

With Annie and Charles as our first guest sitters apported flowers included a red dahlia for Annie, a red and orange gaillardia, and a marguerite.

The trumpet moved immediately we started. Spirit visitors included May Shaw who was one of Charles's daughters from his first marriage. Sunrise did his usual job as linkman. Aunt Agg and Sam both spoke very clearly, but the 'event' of the evening was when two of my mother's sisters Lily and Esther sang a delightful duet through the trumpet, which was enjoyed by us all. My mother told me afterwards that this was something they used to do regularly before their passing to Spirit - similar to what she and Doris also did for the church concerts. Before we closed, Aunt Agg told us they had managed to materialise some fingertips and we would get full materialisations later. Great news. Good progress.

Annie and Charles were very pleased with their sitting.

3rd Aug. (14)

Not so much activity with the trumpet as they were experimenting with materialisation. We all clearly heard tapping on the fireplace. Apports included a very old penny out of my box of coins in our house. We knew it was the same penny as it had a nick out of the side and when I checked on returning home it had gone from the box. We also had a spray of pink carnations, a rose for my mother and two carnations for me (my birthday was the next week) from 'Auntie Grandma' who was this week's new Spirit visitor. She spoke to me through the trumpet to say she had come a long way just to speak to me, and Granddad was with her. We called her 'Auntie Grandma' because when Granddad's first wife Esther, mother of their 11 children, passed over he married her sister Agnes who had been Auntie Agnes and thus became 'Auntie Grandma'.

Sunrise spoke and warned us that as my mother's health was not too good at present we should not expect too much for the next few weeks.

10ᵗʰ Aug. (15)

Slow to start this week but carnations and a marguerite were apported. Taps were heard on the fireplace and Sunrise said they would try to show us the materialised fingertips next week in the light of the paint on the trumpets. Sam and Sydney's father spoke, both quite clearly.

17ᵗʰ Aug. (16)

Apports included a variegated carnation, a spray of pink carnations and a 'Crusader' badge, which was left on top of the clock on the mantelpiece. The Crusader Association was a countrywide group linked with the Spiritualist Lyceum and we were intrigued to find out, hopefully next week, to whom the badge belonged and where it had come from. Doris's mother, Annie Hudson, had recently started a trumpet Circle in her house and we had her trumpet in our Circle tonight to see if our Spirit helpers could energise it. It was moved instantly and was then put inside the wooden trumpet and both were lifted together. Sunrise told us my mother's mother, Esther was there but was unable to control the trumpet and speak - she had been passed over since 1900 when my mother was five years old.

More taps on the mantelpiece but there was not sufficient luminosity from the trumpets to show the fingertips. Sunrise asked us to paint a larger white plaque on one side of the wooden trumpet. They had tried to write on the pad alongside me on the hearth but it kept moving, so we were asked to stabilise it - which I did for next week.

Sam spoke very clearly and at length, to tell us how he had felt when he had passed over suddenly on the previous Christmas Day. It was not painful or difficult - just like waking from a sleep. He found everyone on the Other Side so very helpful to him. Because Sydney had taken Sam to one of Helen Duncan's materialisation Circles in Middlesbrough in 1938, his slight knowledge of Spiritualism had helped him enormously. A very good talk and very clear diction.

24th Aug. (17)

Sydney had now painted a three-inch wide strip with white paint on one side of the wooden trumpet. (Luminous paint was not available so soon after the war). There were immediate taps on the fireplace. The wooden trumpet was lifted from the floor and moved slowly in front of the sitters to enable each one to see the two materialised ectoplasmic hands in front of the white plaque. We were told the hands were those of Aunt Agg and Ivy Hudson. Ivy was Doris's sister who had passed over when she was just one year old in 1922, and was now growing up in Spirit. There was a distinct difference in the sizes.

Shortly afterwards we heard the pencil writing on the paper alongside me on a small table. Sydney had made a solid board and the paper was fixed to it so it could not move. Two asters and two carnations were brought - one for each of the ladies. We asked Sunrise about the last week's badge. He said he could tell us about it but thought it would be better proof to say nothing for now and we would find out eventually.

Sam spoke for just a minute or two to say he had signed his name but Gladys would have to look for it! When the light went on there were signatures on the paper for the first time, Jack, Agnes, Mona and Ivy, with Sunrise's 'O' at the top and the bottom had all 'signed in'. Sam's signature was later found on one of the lower tiles on the front of the tiled fireplace - typical Sam and I don't think Gladys wiped that tile for a long time!

My notebook says: "A very good evening with boundless possibilities for the future."

31ˢᵗ Aug. (18)

Guest sitter - Marjorie Newton, Sydney's niece.

Immediate taps on fireplace. Wooden trumpet moved after five minutes showing a materialised hand holding a carnation, which was handed directly to Marjorie! Found later it was Mona Hildred's hand.

When Sunrise spoke Sydney asked him how long ago he had passed over: "Too long ago to count" was the reply. Sunrise asked that Mam should sit in Annie Hudson's Circle and then he could advise on the position of their sitters. Sam spoke very clearly; followed by Sydney's father who asked that his widow should come to the circle. Sydney said he would arrange it.

A colleague in the office told me on the Friday that his father had passed over that afternoon and asked me whether he could receive help in the Spirit World. I put the question to Sunrise without giving any names. He immediately responded by saying they could help him and went on to tell me that my colleague's name was James Arthur Wright - exactly the same as his father's. I found that to be correct when I checked with Jimmy on the Monday!

Four more carnations were apported for Marjorie and Gladys' belt was apported from the passage. Sunrise said my mother's health was improving and we could ask guests to sit with us, within reason.

An excellent sitting all round.

7ᵗʰ Sept. (19)

Mam had a heavy cold so we did not expect much phenomena yet the trumpets both moved very quickly. Sam materialised his hand and hit the wooden trumpet with terrific force. He appeared to be very excited and then touched Mrs H on the knee. An exciting demonstration of Spirit and psychic energy.

Douglas Hildred then whistled through the trumpet but was unable to speak. Sunrise explained he would have to learn to speak as he passed over when only 5 days old, 16 years before. (He did gradually learn to speak and we then had many interesting conversations with him, one very special one, which I have on the tape recording of the Christmas Party sitting in January 1954.)

Aunt Agg spoke - first time for many weeks, as she had been very busy looking after her husband, Uncle Bob, who had just passed over. Apported flowers - two chrysanths, one aster, one dahlia. More signatures on the paper - Margaret, Sunrise's two 'O's and some scribbles (from children).

A rather quiet evening but still good. Who is Margaret? A question for next week.

14ᵗʰ Sept. (20)

Taps on fireplace. Apported flowers - chrysanth, single aster, double aster and french marigold. Sam was delighted to be able to materialise his two hands and move both trumpets around the room. We were delighted when he signalled that we could touch his hands without affecting the 'conditions'. They felt quite warm and natural, exactly the same as our own hands. Wonderful - here we were actually feeling the materialised hands of someone who was now in the Spirit World - with more to come !

Aunt Agg spoke, clearly but quietly. She said Mam's throat was not too good so it was difficult to talk through the trumpet. Very pleased with our progress and told us her daughter's baby, who had passed over soon after childbirth, was there with her. Uncle Bob was improving as he now realised he had passed over. She also told us we could ask two longstanding Spiritualist friends next week - Lily Dinsdale and George Gills.

Sunrise spoke to let us know he also was pleased with our progress.

The answer to our question about Margaret was given in writing on the sheet of paper which showed the name 'Hanking', who was the first wife of my mother's brother Alb.

21ˢᵗ Sept. (21)

Guest sitters - Lily Dinsdale and George Gills.

Apported flowers - rose and carnation for Lily, chrysanth for George and a carnation for the Circle. Lily's mother's hand materialised and showed itself in front of the trumpet. It then hit the trumpet and finally handed one of the carnations directly to Lily. Both Lily and her mother showed signs of excitement. George's young daughter, Alice, materialised her hand in front of the trumpet and tapped it. Sam then got hold of both trumpets, same as last week, but much more easily. Alice then spoke to George - fairly clearly which was quite good for the first time - followed by her mother Dora who said her throat was still rather sore which made it difficult. Dora had passed over with TB, which had seriously affected her throat.

Lily's mother spoke to her. Sunrise took over the trumpet to let Sam speak, who was followed by Uncle Jack, the first time he had spoken for many weeks. The Spirit children ended the sitting by ringing the 'crinoline lady' bell and moving all the things on the mantelpiece.

Signatures on the paper - Dora and Alice, we gave the sheet of paper to George of course.

An excellent sitting, both guests were extremely happy and grateful.

28th Sept. (22)

Apported flowers - two chrysanths for Doris and five purple asters for me. Very slow at first but Doris saw something in front of the plaque. Sunrise told us it was one of his feathers and they were now trying to get us Spirit lights. He then answered questions about Annie Hudson's Circle and was satisfied with their progress.

We asked about the possibility of an infrared photograph showing how the trumpet was moved. He told us he would have to put Mam into trance for that and we would have to wait a little longer. (I can tell you now that 'a little longer' turned out to be more than two years, to ensure my mother's safety!) He also said that Lily Dinsdale would make a good trumpet medium (which months later proved correct) and that Mam had gastric influenza and needed rest.

5th Oct. (23)

Guest sitter Sydney's mother, Mrs Shipman, who was very hard of hearing.

Sunrise explained that they were especially using the power for the benefit of Mrs Shipman. Her husband who had been passed over a few years, picked up the trumpets, showed his materialised hand holding a carnation and then handed it to Mrs S. Then he hit the trumpet to show how solid he was, and hit Mrs S on the knee three times.

He then took the trumpet across to close beside Mrs Shipman's ear and spoke very loudly. Sunrise came through very loud and told my father his chest trouble needed plenty of rest and they would help as much as possible. He also gave us a message from Uncle Jack to say he had not forgotten the Wedding Anniversary that coincided with the night we had guest sitters and would bring some flowers another week. This was another example of how our Spirit friends are in close touch with us and still remember anniversaries. Aunt Agg showed her materialised hand and two chrysanths were apported

for the Circle. Plenty of power well used for Mrs
Shipman's benefit.

12ᵗʰ Oct. (24)

Feeling of great power. A spray of Michaelmas' daisies
was placed on my lap and I learned later they came from
Uncle Jack for good luck, as I was considering changing
jobs. Uncle Jack materialised his hand and arm and tapped
me on my head before touching my mother and father.
Very good indeed! Sunrise spoke and introduced two new
Spirit friends, Mr and Mrs Batten, who also spoke through
the trumpet. Doris's Aunt Ada spoke, clearly but faintly.

Uncle Jack then spoke to say he had brought the
flowers for his widow and we found them on the hearth at
the end of the sitting - a lovely bouquet of two roses, two
carnations, two chrysanths and some greenery - which I
delivered the following day. He passed on family messages
before Topsy and Sammy spoke to us (two of the Spirit
children attached to the circle). Sunrise closed by saying
we should soon be seeing the Spirit lights.

Good news and an excellent sitting.

19ᵗʰ Oct. (25)

At the very beginning three chrysanths were dropped,
one each on the knees of Gladys, Mrs Hildred and Sydney.
Trumpets were manipulated inside each other to try to get
enough power to show Spirit lights. Sunrise explained
there was not quite sufficient power but hopefully next
week we would see them inside the trumpets. Douglas
Hildred, who had passed over as a baby, had been learning,
from his father, how to speak and spoke to us for a few
minutes, slowly but quite clearly. Excellent progress. Two
new Spirit visitors also spoke through the trumpet and
then Sam spoke for over five minutes with great control.
Mam had felt discomfort in her stomach during the day
and Sunrise told her it was nothing serious, only that they
were taking 'energy' ready for the evening sitting. Sydney

had felt a lot of pain in his ankle during the sitting and Sunrise told him it was rheumatism but would soon clear up. Sunrise also told us that there was another visitor from the Spirit World - a Mr Gibson, who wanted to give a message that "they had not forgotten the wee lassie's birthday and Archie is with us."

We had known the Gibson family for many years - true Scots, but we knew nothing of their daughters' birth dates. When we called to pass on the message to one of the ladies she confirmed that it had been her birthday that very Saturday. Excellent evidence again with no possible explanation of it being 'mind-reading'.

Good sitting again, still showing good progress.

26ᵗʰ Oct. (26)

One of very few sittings I missed through illness - in bed with influenza this time. The notes were made by Gladys and it seems I missed another exceptional sitting when Spirit lights were seen for the first time. Four lights lasting three or four seconds at about one minute intervals. Fortunately for me this was not a one-off happening and we had many more lights for many weeks ahead. A new visitor announced himself as Edward Brownie (known to us from then on as Brownie) speaking with perfect clarity in a Cockney dialect. He had been a barrow boy, a London street urchin, living on his wits, who had passed over through an accident about 50 years before. He had been 'summoned' by Sunrise to come and help with some healing for me and for our four children. He gave a favourable report and spoke about his life for about 10 minutes.

Let me now add that he became a very close Spirit helper, particularly for healing and apports, and is still around occasionally even now, over 50 years later. They never forget us when in need.

A carnation was shown against the plaque; a rose and two chrysanths were found later.

Sam spoke for about five minutes and told us news of the reception in the Spirit World given for Mr Troughton, a neighbour of Sam and Mrs Hildred. Topsy, a Spirit child helper, also spoke for a few minutes saying she could speak as well as Sunrise.

Sunrise concluded by saying my energy had still been present and when Doris got home she was to look in the bedroom for a flower, which they had taken for me! I well remember her returning home and looking round the bedroom for something, which I knew nothing about. After a few minutes she looked under a corner of the eiderdown on the bed and found a lovely carnation - possibly the one shown in front of the plaque. This was a wonderful surprise and was the first time an apport had been taken from the Circle room to an outside place, although we had a few more similar happenings over the years ahead. A very exciting and significant event.

2nd Nov. (27)

This sitting was unusual in that we had five members of Mrs Hudson's Circle as guests, to help them to appreciate what physical phenomena was like.

Apart from Mrs Hudson they had not experienced such rare phenomena and we hoped their visit would give them help and encouragement for their development. We had lots of different phenomena including flowers for some of the guests, materialised hands, four Spirit lights and five people speaking through the trumpet, but I was delighted when Sunrise let Brownie speak, whom I had missed last week. Very clear speech and called himself a "rough card."

He stayed quite a while and told us he had brought a badge from Mrs Hudson's kitchen. Her son Clive, who was a member of their Circle, spoke, and Brownie said he knew him because he had seen him washing in the kitchen and took the badge from the window ledge thinking it was Clive's. When we saw it at the end of the sitting it turned out to be a metal school 'Captain's' badge actually belonging to Clive's younger sister Janet, who was still at school. A very interesting apport and it was easy to see why Brownie had thought it belonged to Clive, who was coming to our Circle that night. Brownie also helped by removing a severe colic pain, which I had when we started sitting.

9th Nov. (28)

Guests - Auntie Nain and Uncle Levy (relatives of Mrs Hildred) and a long-standing church member and good medium Mrs Kay.

It was a very rainy night and the apported flowers, three chrysanths and one rose were very weather-beaten. They must have been 'picked' from an outdoor garden. Three Spirit lights brighter than last week. Mrs Kay's sister materialised her hand but was unable to speak through the trumpet. Sunrise gave her name as Helena, which was absolutely correct and was a good test for Mrs Kay. Sam had his usual chat with his relatives and signed his name on the paper this time. Then another lovely surprise when Brownie took over the trumpet direct from Sam, whereas normally Sunrise acted as an intermediary. He said there were still ill health conditions around and I was not fully fit, so he would probably 'drop in' for the next couple of weeks and then move on to help another Circle!

A very good sitting and we were given permission to have a red light next week. We had been asking about such a possibility and were delighted to receive such permission for a dim light at first. It was a flash lamp bulb fixed in a wooden box made by Sydney, with a sheet of red glass on one side and powered by a torch battery. The benefit of it of course, was to be able to see the materialisations more clearly than just in front of the white plaque - and it worked very well. It is interesting to mention that I still have that sheet of red glass and the original flash lamp bulb, which still works more than 50 years later!

23rd Nov. (30)

Before we put on the red light we had 10 beautiful chrysanths apported. Then in the red light, we saw a materialised hand belonging to a sea-faring man called William Ratcliffe, with one finger missing. Sam spoke very clearly and said we would get materialisations as good as Helen Duncan - about which we were naturally extremely thrilled but found hard to believe at this stage. ("Oh ye of little faith" we all murmured!) Sunrise said they would then take Mam into deep trance for such phenomena. On the whole a quiet night but very interesting with the red light for the first time.

30th Nov. (31)

Guest sitter - Mr William Brittain Jones FRCS, who was invited because knowing him slightly we knew of his interest in physical phenomena, and of his integrity as a very highly respected and reputable senior surgeon on Tees-side.

Again before the red light was switched on, we had three chrysanths apported - one for Mr Jones. When the light was on, we saw Mr Jones's mother's materialised hand holding a rose, which she handed directly to him. Quite a thrill for both of them. Sunrise spoke, approved of the light, and gave Mr Jones's mother's name as Mary, which was correct. She then spoke very faintly through the trumpet. Sunrise also told Mr Jones that one of his old colleagues had come to see him - a Doctor Belas who had died with cancer of the gullet ("Absolutely correct" said Mr Jones).

Unfortunately Mam picked up his condition and started coughing violently. The trumpet then dropped to the floor but came up again after three or four minutes - thanks to Sunrise's protection and control. Just before the end Ivy Hudson brought two carnations for her mother's birthday today - which Doris delivered on the Sunday.

A good night, thoroughly enjoyed by Mr Jones who was invited to come again sometime, (meaning sometime in the future). Fortunately for us he misinterpreted the 'sometime', and turned up two weeks later, to our great benefit. We were always delighted and grateful for his 'misinterpretation' - our Spirit team obviously intended him to be part of our Saturday Night Club team, and arranged it accordingly. He soon became a valuable, regular member of our Saturday Night Club and the harmony in the Circle was certainly not altered.

The variety and quality of the phenomena we had been privileged to witness during these first eight months - just 31 sittings, astounded and excited us week by week in an ever increasing intensification, and if we had received nothing more, our lives and our knowledge would still have been greatly enhanced. We never became blasé about our experiences. Each sitting was a new experience, a 'special' occasion, with some perhaps a little 'more special' than others. The joy and thrill of regularly conversing with our loved ones from the Spirit World, having their permanent signatures, receiving their superb apports, witnessing their Spirit lights, fascinated by the amazing gyrations of the trumpets - all this, and much more important, the simple fact of being an integral part of such a wonderful 'family gathering' of like minds from both Worlds.

But as the man said years later - "You ain't seen nothing yet!" - and how true that was for the Saturday Night Club from Sitting 32.

9

A Breathtaking Experience

We had been sitting for only eight months when during Sitting 32 on 7th Dec. 1946 we were astounded to have such a phenomenal and breathtaking experience; truly 'out of this world'. We met our first fully formed ectoplasmic materialised Spirit person! It may not have been as grandiose or stupendous as Spielberg's block-buster film, 'Close Encounters of the Third Kind' many years later, but for us it was amazingly awe-inspiring in a far more intimate manner.

Here in this everyday friendly sitting room adjacent to Sydney and Gladys' shop, with the door and windows locked, we opened and closed our Sitting that evening with *seven* of us round the fireplace, yet, for a few precious minutes during that Sitting there were *eight* of us, all clearly visible to each other in the red light which illuminated the room during the whole Sitting of some 45 minutes. The eighth person who joined us for that brief time was none other than Aunt Agg, who had been in the Spirit World for almost four years, since November 1942.

Firstly let me remind you that ectoplasm is not a 'ghostly, vapour-like' substance, which simply floats around the atmosphere. It is a tangible, transmutative material produced by the Spirit chemists/scientists from within the body of the medium. How they produce it cannot be explained by our current scientific terminology - in the same way that I could not explain or describe to a person blind from birth, any colour in the spectrum. But let me assure you they do create it in the medium and it emanates from one or more orifices such as the mouth, nostrils, ears or solar plexus. In my mother's mediumship it generally came from the mouth, as will be seen from the infrared photograph in this book.

On this particular evening we sat in the red light with my mother in full view of everyone in the room, sitting on her usual dining chair at the end of the semi-circle of sitters around the fireplace. I always sat immediately opposite her at the other end of the semi-circle and could clearly see anything that happened. We sat for at least half an hour and nothing had happened - which was most unusual. We were beginning to think there would be no phenomena that evening, when we saw this white disc, about two feet diameter, on the floor between my mother and myself.

Because of the smallness of the room I was never more than five feet from my mother and could clearly see this white disc, which was linked to my mother, who was now in deep trance control and knew nothing about what was happening. As you will have read from the previous chapters, we had seen and felt ectoplasmic hands but had never seen such a large quantity of ectoplasm. We were all very excited of course and as we chatted we saw this disc begin to build into a vertical white column, which grew to about five feet of solid ectoplasm! "Amazing" we said!

We then expected the column to simply gradually diminish and let the ectoplasm return to my mother - but that did not happen. The column remained still for a few minutes whilst we all stared at it, getting more and more excited. Then, as I was watching it, the top of it twisted towards me and I could just see there was the semblance of a face in it, but I could not have recognised who it was.

From the body of the column there then appeared two hands and arms covered by the ectoplasmic 'robes' of the person who was standing in front of me. As the hands approached me, I instinctively stretched out my arms and hands towards them - not in any way frightened as it all seemed so natural, but still a little apprehensive I suppose, about meeting a materialised Spirit person so close for the first time.

Our hands engaged and I then realised that in my right hand I was being given four beautiful carnations, apports. As I grasped the flowers very tightly, my two hands were firmly clasped by the warm ectoplasmic hands in front of me. I then heard, quietly but clearly, from the face above me, the words "For you, for you,". The hands and arms went back into the 'column' of ectoplasm and it then shrunk, slowly towards the floor, as the ectoplasm returned to my mother and we were all left exceedingly breathless after such a unique experience.

As for me, there I was sitting on my chair opposite my mother, with my mouth wide open, still tightly grasping the four carnations I had received a few moments before, trying to appreciate the full meaning of my 'brief encounter' of a most wonderful kind!

We later learned that our first visitor had been Aunt Agg, who because of her mediumistic qualities and empathy with her sister often became the 'test pilot'. I still found it difficult to comprehend fully the significance of her visit, but there was no question about her presence as confirmed by the beautiful carnations I was still grasping many minutes afterwards. We shared them amongst us and mine still has prime position in my folder of Memorabilia.

10

'S N C' - Sittings Nos. 33 to 43

For the next five sittings we had many materialised
Spirit people standing with us in the middle of that room,
in a red light, by the fireplace, alongside my mother who
was in deep trance. As you will observe, fantastic progress
was made during these sittings and if I had not actually
been there to witness such phenomena, I could have found
it very difficult to accept. But I *was* there and had no
difficulty whatsoever in accepting what happened.

14ᵗʰ Dec. (33)

Sam Hildred materialised and handed Mrs H. a lovely
orchid. Mr Jones mother built, rather weak, but was able
to shake hands with him and finally called him "Brittain,
my boy", which delighted Mr Jones as this was the name
she often used on the earth. Aunt Agg built and greeted
everyone by moving round the sitters and shaking hands.
An excellent materialised form and Mr Jones was very
impressed. Sunrise closed by saying we could try a
brighter red light next week – but no promises. While we
were having supper afterwards Mr Jones said he would
have liked to have tested her pulse. We told him we would
ask next week, assuming Aunt Agg would be coming.

21ˢᵗ Dec. (34)

We started with a brighter light, but as my mother had
a cold and bad throat, after 20 minutes Sunrise controlled
her and said we would have to reduce the light, which I
promptly did. Sam built again, much clearer, and handed

Gladys two tulips for her mother who was in bed at home with a severe cold. Then Aunt Agg built and handed me a bunch of violets for her sister, Mary, who was in Middlesbrough on a holiday from Bristol. Before we had time to mention Mr Jones request, she turned towards him and said she understood he would like to feel her pulse.

She had obviously been 'ear-wigging' during supper last week! She pulled back the sleeve of her ectoplasmic robe and proffered her arm towards Mr Jones, who promptly stood up and took the pulse in his professional manner. After about 30 seconds he removed his hand and thanked her very much, adding, dryly, "You'll live!", at which Aunt Agg chuckled and replied "Thank you Mr Jones, I *am* living, and will *continue* to live!"; a very interesting incident, which indicated that Aunt Agg was a solid ectoplasmic person with a sound pulse and was not just a 'ghostly phantom'. This was similar to an experiment, which William Crookes had carried out with medium Florence Cook and the materialised spirit of Katie King around 1874.

When Mr J had finished, Aunt Agg stretched out her right hand towards my father and her left hand towards me and beckoned us to stand alongside her under the red light so we could clearly see and recognise her as the person we had known for so many years on the earth.

Doris's sister, Ivy, was the last to build. She seemed a little upset and asked Doris to tell her mother she was helping all she could. We were not aware of any problem but obviously Ivy was concerned and wanted her mother to know she was around.

From this week onwards we decided we would close the sitting when my mother came out of trance.

28ᵗʰ Dec. (35)

28ᵗʰ Dec. (35)

Guests – Mrs Shipman (Sydney's mother), their relatives John Newton and Marjorie, and my mother's sister Mary, on holiday from Bristol.

Aunt Agg built first to greet her sister, who in her young days was an excellent mental medium. She then spoke to and shook hands with John and Marjorie. Granny Newton followed – joined John and Marjorie's hands and gave them a chrysanth. Granny Lumsden came for Doris, held her hand and said they were doing all they could to help. Mr Shipman then built, took hold of Sydney and Mrs Shipman's hands but was unable to speak much.

The last to build was my father's mother, Grandma Harrison, who stood Dad and me up, one each side of her, in the middle of the room. Keeping hold of our hands she said, "God bless you" to my father and called me "Sonny", by which name I was known to the family for many years and the only name ever used by Grandma before her passing to the Spirit World. Sunrise spoke again just to say "Farewell", (a new word for him). Excellent progress with five splendid materialisations.

4ᵗʰ Jan. 1947 (36)

Guests, Aunt Mary and Mrs Urwin, the wife of Mr Jones's closest surgeon colleague at the hospital.

Sam built, gave Gladys a chrysanth and held her hand very tightly. Aunt Agg came again, spoke very clearly, gave Aunt Mary a chrysanth, walked round the room, shook hands with Mrs Irwin, Mr Jones and my father. I was able to feel her gossamer-like robe, which was beautifully soft. I asked her whether Uncle Jack could come to meet his sister Mary – which he did next, but could not stay long and was only able to say "Hello, Mary" – but at least they met face to face. Mr Jones's mother then built quite clearly called him "Britt my boy", and he introduced her to Mrs Irwin. Mrs Irwin's grandmother then built but unfortunately was not strong enough to speak. Sunrise told us the power had gone and would we sing for the Spirit children before we closed – which we did of course.

11ᵗʰ Jan. (37)

Only the original six sitters tonight as both Mrs H. and Mr J. were away.

We started at 8 pm with the brighter light again and nothing happened until 8.45 pm when Sunrise controlled my mother to say the light was still too bright without a cabinet. (See explanation later). We dimmed it and continued to sit. Mona Hildred built very clearly to bring Gladys a flower for their mother's birthday that very day. My father's father built clearly but could not speak much. Doris's Aunt Ada then came to give her a carnation. Finally Sam Hildred built and gave Gladys a carnation for his wife's birthday.

Special note – before we dimmed the red light Sunrise said he would try to show us the ectoplasm coming from my mother. We soon saw a white mass in front of my mother's stomach, which gradually extended for about 12 inches, stayed for three or four minutes and then gradually went back and disappeared; a very interesting and instructive experiment.

Sunrise then commented on two other matters. Firstly, since Sitting 32 we had had no trumpet voices, only materialisations, and he said we could have the trumpet again whenever we wished without any special notice or preparation. Secondly, we could have a brighter light for the materialised forms if my mother was 'partitioned off', sitting behind a curtain in a cabinet. A cabinet, in séance terms, is usually a tall, four sided enclosure in which the medium sits. The front of it has a curtain, which can be drawn or held back by the Spirit people when necessary.

We thanked him for that excellent news and by the following week Sydney had fixed a long piece of blackout curtain to a wooden pole, which rested on the picture rail across the corner to the left hand side of the fireplace to create a simple cabinet. The space above the pole to the ceiling caused them no problems and that acted as our cabinet for all the years we sat.

The advantage of using the cabinet was that the Spirit people materialised in the semi-darkness, which used less power, and then simply moved the curtain sideways with their materialised arms to show themselves standing by the side of the fireplace. It also meant that more Spirits would be able to build and stay longer in the brighter red light.

But it was another five months before Aunt Agg was actually able to walk out, away from the curtain of the cabinet, for about three feet into the room, during Sitting No.60. But I emphasise here again, that wherever the ectoplasmic forms moved around the room, they were always connected to my mother behind the curtain, by means of an ectoplasmic cord emanating from her body. Hence the need for the vouchsafing of our guest sitters who were always strongly advised about the dangers to the medium if any untoward actions were taken by the sitters.

Let me say now, that thankfully, we never had to deal with any such problems being caused by any of the two hundred plus guests over the many years of our sittings – and they always commented on the naturalness and homeliness of the whole evening.

18ᵗʰ Jan. (38)

First sitting with the cabinet, which was used from this week onwards. Tried with brighter light but had to dim it this time on request from Sunrise. First to build was Granny Harrison, my father's grandmother who stayed a few minutes but was unable to speak. Aunt Agg followed, standing just free of the curtain alongside the fireplace. As I went over to meet her I talked to her about them signing their names on the sheet of paper and asked her whether she could perhaps sign her name in my notebook using my pen. After a little hesitation and chuckle, she said she had not held a pen for many years but would see what she could do. She took my pen in her hand, I held my notebook in front of her, and she signed her name – Agnes; splendid evidence of her physical presence in an ectoplasmic body.

Uncle Jack came later, shook hands with everyone and told me he would sign his name next week! After Uncle Jack went, Sam Hildred built for a few minutes and finally Uncle Jack came back to hand me two Chrysanths for his daughter's birthday on the 23rd Jan. It was particularly interesting that he called her by his nickname for her - "Bun", real name Bessie. I was delighted to take them to her on the Sunday.

25th Jan (39)

Guest – Mrs Shipman. First materialisation was Mr Shipman who handed two tulips to his wife. Ivy Hudson then built and brought a tulip for her father's birthday today, which Doris was delighted to take to him the next day. Sunrise then said there was a gentleman present who was unable to build but gave the initials "J.J.", followed by "Thompson", who was recognised by Mr Jones as the District Tuberculosis Officer from Darlington. His message to Mr J. was that he was "on the right lines", which pleased Mr J. greatly, as this was only his third sitting, and now a regular member of our Circle. Aunt Agg came for her usual chat and Mr Jones felt her pulse again. Sunrise said there was only enough power left for one more and Sam and Uncle Jack had to decide who would come. Sam kindly agreed to Uncle Jack coming so he could sign his name – which he did. He did comment that it didn't feel like his hand, which I suppose was quite likely as he had been passed over for almost 20 years. Fortunately Sam was still able to build for a few moments and Mrs Hildred kissed him. She said his face felt 'quite flesh like'; another splendid evening.

1st Feb (40)

Sam materialised immediately bringing two tulips and a carnation for Gladys' birthday the next day. I also asked him if he would like to sign my book, which he did without any problem. Those three signatures are still clearly visible in my notebook. Granny Lumsden then built and gave Doris three chrysanths. Esther Bessant, another of mother's sisters, built very clearly, and spoke with a lovely clear voice. Mr Charles Roeder, who had been well known to us all as Middlesbrough Church President and Conductor of the Lyceum, built in the cabinet but was not strong enough to come into the red light.

8th Feb (41)

Guest - Jimmy Wright (a work colleague of mine). We started tonight with the trumpet, the first time for two months. Sunrise introduced Jimmy's father who tried to speak but not very clearly. Aunt Agg materialised at the end of the sitting and handed four tulips to Jimmy from his father. Jimmy was naturally very thrilled. (see Sitting 18.)

15th Feb (42)

Sunrise and Sam both spoke through the trumpet, each for about 10 minutes. Sam was explaining about the different planes in the Spirit World - as he said, like Middlesbrough and Redcar, a seaside resort about 10 miles away, so you can visit other people but aren't always very close to each other. Later, Mr Charles Roeder (past President, Middlesbrough Church) materialised. He invited us all to feel his beard, which felt very natural. Three tulips were on the floor when we switched on the light.

22nd Feb (43)

This turned out to be a memorable sitting. After three Spirit visitors had spoken through the trumpet, my mother's father, Granddad Bessant, materialised. So this was a very special occasion for me. Granddad had passed almost 30 years earlier, when I was only a few months old, and although he had nursed me, talked to me and showed me much affection I had no recollection of him. Now here he was a tall, upright man complete with dark moustache and full beard. I walked across to him and felt his strong grip as we held hands, hands much larger than my mother's. A very emotional moment for us both, I suppose. He stayed and talked for about 3 minutes and I cannot recall what we said to each other, until just before he was going he said, "Feel my beard, my boy, feel my beard." I reached up, for he was taller than me, and felt this very soft 'hair', which was, of course, ectoplasm in yet another form. It was not unlike Mr Roeder's last week, but much denser and the hairs much longer; another exceptional experience.

When we told my mother after the sitting she was as thrilled as I and commented that he had always been very proud of his beard and had tended it daily, hence his request for me to feel it. So his physical appearance was still as important to him now as it had been before his passing and he wanted me to share it with him.

As you are reading these very brief records of our remarkable experiences, I truly hope you are able to sense and share with us the deeply felt excitement and thrill which pervaded every one of our Sittings in Sydney and Gladys' homely sitting room. Each week was different in content of course, but each week was special - very special in fact. We never took anything for granted, nor became the slightest bit blasé, even after several years of our weekly get-togethers with our Spirit friends - as was the original intent and purpose of our Saturday Night Club.

It had certainly grown and developed far beyond our highest hopes and dreams, but it still remained the very same informal, cheerful and chatty gathering of friends and relatives from both worlds. Extremely privileged we certainly were, and even now, 50 years later, those finer feelings are still as strong within me.

11

Granny Lumsden

Granny was Doris's grandmother on her mother's side. Doris's mother Annie and father Charles were frequent guests in our Home Circle, and all three of them were absolutely sure that the materialised person they met so often was undoubtedly the same person they knew and loved when she was on the earth plane. Their conversations about family affairs from years gone by proved the lady standing there amongst us was the same mother and grandmother. I had met Granny a number of times with Doris in our schooldays, and remembered her as the small, very lively and active lady who lived next door to Jim McKenzie and family, whose three children were good friends of ours.

It was the same Jim McKenzie who, on 18th October 1947, took the first two quarter-plate photographs of our materialised Spirit people and Granny had the 'honour' of being first, with Aunt Agg second, on the same evening. He also made the reel-to-reel tape recording of our special Christmas party sitting in 1954. This treasured recording includes a few minutes of Granny chatting away in her inimitable, cheerful style with her typical Middlesbrough accent, which, when I play it at the end of my talks, arouses great interest and much laughter from the audiences.

Granny was obviously interested in psychic matters as we have one of Billy Hope's spirit photographs taken in Mr and Mrs Hudson's home, 87 Ayresome Park Road,

Middlesbrough in 1927, showing Granny as one of the sitters.

One of Granny's daughters, Ada, passed over in childbirth leaving Cyril, a day old baby to be cared for. Typically, Granny, then 73, took him to her home and although he was a 'sickly bairn' she successfully reared him for his first two years before her passing to the Spirit World in 1930 aged 75.

In the early months of Cyril's life Doris, who was still at school, used to stay at Granny's each night to help look after him. Her particular job, during the night, was to heat his bottle over the gas flame in the bedroom! As there was no electricity in the house it meant Doris having to go up the dark staircase with a spluttering candle for illumination.

Not very pleasant for a 12 year old girl and on one occasion she had her first experience of clairvoyance when, at the top of the stairs she saw, clearly, Cyril's mother standing there, smiling. It was a bit of a shock for her but knowing about the Spirit World, she quickly realised Aunt Ada was letting her know that she was around helping to care for her child, and Doris was therefore never afraid to climb that dark staircase by herself.

Granny first materialised at our circle in December 1946 (Sitting 35) and then just occasionally during the next 10 months, but from October 1947 she became the first of the five or six materialised people to come during each sitting. She laughingly introduced herself as the 'warm-up' woman to one of our guests, and she was certainly that, with a chuckle and cheery word for each sitter as she walked round the room in a good red light.

Comments like "Are you enjoying it love" made the guests feel quite at home and helped remove any tension they may have felt, although at the end of every sitting they always commented how natural the whole evening had been, but there is one particular occurrence during one of our sittings, which deserves special mention. On this particular occasion Granny had introduced herself to a lady guest and then most unexpectedly asked her if she would like to feel her feet. This certainly took me by surprise - why her feet?

When greeting her, Doris and I regularly held her hands, which were always as warm as our own, so I immediately asked her why she wanted the lady to feel her feet.

"Well," she said, "I always had cold feet when I lived here." My prompt response was to say that she couldn't have cold feet now in the Spirit World without a physical body. "That's right," she said, "Only when I get into this stuff!" She was referring to the ectoplasmic body, which she laughingly called 'this stuff' - typical Granny. So I left my chair and knelt down beside her - I wanted to check her statement for myself and give support to the lady guest. I asked her to lift one of her feet and cupped it in my hands. It was just like a block of ice, yet her hands were quite warm! I made some appropriate comment and all Granny said was "I told you so!" The lady guest also felt her foot and confirmed my comment.

She did what we laughingly called 'her party piece' three or four times over the next few weeks, always with the same result - her feet were ice cold. One week when we had no guests and Granny was standing talking to us, I said, "Are your feet still cold this week, Gran?"

Her reply rather surprised me - "No, not this week." My immediate response was "You said whenever you were in this stuff you had cold feet, so why not tonight?" "Well you have no guests." "What difference does that make to your feet?" I asked. "Well as you have no guests tonight I haven't bothered to bring my feet!!!" That really shook us all. There she was walking around the room but without any feet - and just to prove her word, she bent forward, lifted her ectoplasmic robe to her waist and there were no feet or legs! I could see my Dad's legs the other side of the room beneath her robe. Granny was right again, she hadn't bothered to bring her feet! So how was she walking around the room?

We soon had the answer from Aunt Agg, who explained that the ectoplasm was simply a material covering for the Spirit or Ethereal body, which takes up no space but can be used as a 'vehicle' for moving around. Furthermore, the Spirit people cover with ectoplasm only the parts of the Spirit body, which they need at that time - and Granny did not need her feet for her 'party piece' as we had no guests.

Aunt Agg also explained that the 'production' of the ectoplasm uses a 'portion' of the total 'energy' or 'power' available in the Circle each evening, which is not limitless but varies with the conditions emanating from the sitters and the climatic conditions that evening. The less energy that is used for each individual materialisation means that more Spirit people are able to materialise and that they can stay for longer periods. As Aunt Agg succinctly put it with a lovely chuckle, "The more the merrier for all of us." They are so keen to let us know they are still living happily in a much better world and are often around us, particularly in times of need.

Thanks to Granny we all learned something that evening. Our Spirit friends are not subject to the laws of physics or chemistry as set down on the earth plane. It is a great pity that the scientists here cannot accept this proven Truth of Life after Death. Those reputable and creditable men, like William Crookes, Oliver Lodge, Arthur Conan Doyle and others, who, when they publicly declared their favourable findings, were disowned by their colleagues who considered they 'had lost their marbles'. All very sad but the Truth can never be destroyed; it lives on - and on - and on, which they will all discover when their time comes to join their colleagues in the Spirit World.

12

'S N C' - Sittings Nos. 44 Onwards

In the previous chapters I have detailed most of the early Sittings, but from hereon I shall extract only those, which I consider to have particularly interesting or have significant happenings not covered elsewhere. Let me remind you that each sitting lasted over an hour and we always had our usual six, seven or more Spirit visitors, either speaking through the trumpet or materialising, usually bringing apported flowers for their relatives or friends. Make no mistake, every sitting, each week, was always 'special'.

1ˢᵗ March 1947 (44)
No guests, just the original six sitters.
Sunrise promised us all that he would arrange for each of our main guides to speak to us soon and he would materialise during *Sitting 52* - on our first Anniversary.

8ᵗʰ March (45)
Guest, Mrs Shipman (Syd's mother)
Sunrise, Syd's father and Sam Hildred all spoke clearly through the trumpet. Tulips were apported for Gladys and Mrs Shipman, Mimosa for Doris and Sydney.
First materialisation was Syd's guide who announced himself as John Evans, a Methodist Minister from Cardiff in 1885. He had a full beard but was 'thin on top'. Mr Shipman came next and stayed a while to talk to his widow. Aunt Agg then built with advice for Terry about his work and forthcoming marriage.

22nd March (47)

Our first sitting using a rheostat, made by Mr Garrett, a friend of Sydney's, which I was able to use for varying the brightness of the ruby-red light for the materialisations. Those, like Aunt Agg, were able to stand a brighter light, whereas the 'first-timers' needed a much dimmer light. Over the ensuing years we found this equipment extremely useful. The Spiritualist Pioneer, Alfred Kitson built. Such a special occasion that this has warranted its own chapter following this one.

29th March (48)

Guest - Sam Ingham, whose wife Ethel materialised and handed him a white carnation with a white/pink tulip. She apologised for being unable to bring exactly the same flowers she had in her wedding bouquet, which were white tulips; just another example of the closeness of our Spirit friends and relatives. When Aunt Agg built we were all invited to feel the wonderful garments she was wearing - beautifully soft, silk-like ectoplasmic robes.

5th April (49)

Through the trumpet Sunrise told us there was a Spirit lady with a name like a man - Samuel Davies, who wished to materialise later. Doris and I immediately recognised the name as that of the lady we had lived with during my time at the RE Training Centre in Ruabon in 1942/3. As a Sergeant I had been allowed to 'live out' and Doris had come with baby Colin to stay for a few months. We knew her as Mrs Davies, but she was previously married to a Mr Samuels - hence the confusion with the names.

Every evening, during our brief stay, she took Colin in her arms, wrapped him in her Welsh shawl and sang him to sleep with Welsh lullabies. When she built tonight she called out our Christian names and gave Doris two tulips. A very evidential meeting with her.

Tonight was Sydney and Gladys' tenth Wedding Anniversary, and when Gladys' father Sam Hildred built he handed her some pink carnations and a blue iris for memory's sake. As I have said so often, our Spirit friends do not forget such important occasions - as we here so often do.

Towards the close, Gladys' main guide, an Italian lady, Carita Mirello, also built and stayed briefly.

12ᵗʰ April (50)

My main guide materialised first - tall, upright man, with black beard and moustache who spoke good English, and gave his name as Achelem El Achem, an ancient Egyptian.

When Aunt Agg built we asked her about cutting off a piece of her ectoplasmic robes sometime and she said it would be safe with Spirit protection and they would arrange it. She then spread her robes across the Circle and they seemed almost endless, covering the whole floor area in front of the fireplace.

19ᵗʰ April (51)

This Sitting lasted from 8 pm until 9.50 pm, some 40 minutes longer than our usual sittings and proved very interesting. Sam Hildred spoke through the trumpet, following two ladies, and stayed for over 10 minutes telling us about life in their world - much the same as in ours - houses, buildings of various styles, concert areas, gardens with all kinds of flowers and plants etc. but all much lighter and brighter as created by the minds of the Spirit people.

Apparently you can have exactly what you want for as long as you want or feel the need for it. It seems that during the 'settling in' period we cling to our earthly life manner and style, but the great majority of us gradually realise we do not need such things in our new life without a physical body, although there is always a small minority who tend to cling to their material needs and take longer to progress on their Spiritual pathways.

26ᵗʰ April (52)
Our First Anniversary, a special night– see Chapter 14

10ᵗʰ May (54)
As I have said previously, my mother, being in a deep trance state, was completely unaware of the materialised Spirit visitors who were in the room - except during this particular sitting. While Aunt Agg was in the room talking to us, we suddenly heard my mother shuffling behind the curtain. Aunt Agg assured us there was nothing to worry about and they would soon settle 'our Min'. Her spirit had temporarily left her body and was actually looking down from the corner of the room, had seen her sister and was trying to get to her as she was standing in front of the curtain. Within a minute the shuffling ceased and the sitting continued.

When we were having our cup of tea and sandwiches after the sitting had closed, Mam suddenly 'announced' that she remembered that she had been up in the corner of the room, and had seen 'our Agg' standing in the room so tried to get to her, but was unable to do so. This confirmed what Aunt Agg had told us during the sitting, but it was the only time my mother ever 'saw' any of our Spirit visitors. Hence our request later for photographs to help my mother understand what we were privileged to experience each week.

24ᵗʰ May (56)
Another first tonight! Sunrise had promised Mr Brittain Jones that, when the Spirit scientists had put in place the necessary protection for the medium, he would be able to cut off a piece of Aunt Agg's ectoplasmic robes. That promise was kept tonight. Aunt Agg was the first to materialise and immediately asked Mr Jones if he had his

scissors handy. He promptly produced them from his pocket, in which he always carried them every Saturday evening ready for such an occasion. Aunt Agg then held out the edge of her robes towards Mr Jones and told him he could cut off a piece about the size of a lady's handkerchief.

As he made the cut we heard a distinct gasp from both my mother, behind the curtain, and Aunt Agg standing amongst us in a good red light, but as Aunt Agg had already told us, the necessary protection had been put in place no harm came to either of them. Sunrise had previously said this was an experiment and he was not sure that the piece of ectoplasm would still be there at the end of the sitting. It was passed around the sitters to feel the texture and then placed on the mantelpiece. It was like very fine silk voile.

Unfortunately it was not there at the end of the sitting, but Sunrise had promised that Mr Jones would be given another opportunity the next week and asked for a small jar to be put on the mantelpiece, and 'Swift' our Spirit chemist would arrange to put in some liquid to keep the piece of ectoplasm for as long as possible.

Important reminder to all members or sitters in a Physical Home Circle: Do nothing untoward when sitting in a physical home circle without the previous permission of your Spirit helpers and guides. As you have just read, both the medium and the ectoplasmic form of Aunt Agg were affected by the cutting of the ectoplasm, even with the cloak of protection in place. Without that protection, in such a heightened state of sensitivity, the result could have been extremely harmful and seriously injurious to the medium. Think and ask before you act.

31ˢᵗ May (57)

Gladys had placed a small empty jar on the mantelpiece and Mr Jones was given another opportunity to cut off a piece of ectoplasm of a similar size. This was immediately put into the jar and the lid screwed on, but it was noticed that there was a bleach-like odour coming from the jar. When the light was put on at the end of the sitting we saw the piece of ectoplasm, this time looking like a piece of very fine cotton material, lying in about an inch of liquid in the jar.

Sydney decided to leave it on the mantelpiece and I called round every day to see what was happening. We observed it gradually dissolving into the liquid, and by the following Wednesday it had completely dissolved, leaving just a few very small wisps in the yellowish liquid.

Mr Jones took the liquid to his hospital laboratory for examination and reported back to us the following Saturday. He had crystallised some of the liquid and found that the crystals closely resembled bleach crystals, which was not unexpected considering the odour from the liquid, but there was nothing else significantly different to indicate the presence of the ectoplasm, which we all found a little disappointing in a strange way.

It was still very intriguing to discover something about the liquid which Swift had apported into the jar - a remarkable feat in itself.

Note: We had guest sitters for both these sittings and I had a confirmatory letter, which is included in the letters chapter, from Mr Bill Lennie who was with us on 24th May and remembered the experiment in great detail.

26th July (65)

Our youngest son, Derek, had been born two days previously so Doris was unable to sit with us tonight. Granny Lumsden materialised, handed me a carnation for 'her lass', Doris, and told us she had also taken some roses to our home in Lambeth Road. She said she had put them on the trolley which stood in the passageway under the staircase, where the 'bairns put their clothes'. When I got home I carefully lifted the clothes on the top of the trolley and found the roses as promised by Granny. Wonderful, apports *outside* the Circle room, and I still have one of them.

Finally Aunt Agg built, sat down on the vacant chair and chatted to us for about 10 minutes - as real and as solid as we are. She also brought flowers for Gladys, Sydney and Mr Jones.

The following week we had the pleasure of Aunt Mary, on holiday from Bristol, as our guest sitter. Aunt Mary was one of my mother's sisters, born in 1883, two years before Aunt Agg and 12 years before my mother. Like all the Bessant family she was very mediumistic, but because of her husband's close links with the Church of England had not kept a close Spirit link since their marriage. So it was particularly interesting for her to sit with us and meet some of the family from the Spirit World.

Her father (my Granddad) came first and gave her a carnation. Albert Ernest, Aunt Mary's first born who passed over as a baby, built next as a tall young man to show his mother how he had progressed. Her mother, who spoke very clearly, then followed - a very bright Spirit who had progressed a long way, according to Sunrise. Finally, Aunt Agg was able to sit on the vacant chair next to her sister and chat about family matters for some 10 minutes. Aunt Agg also handed her a carnation for Aunt Mary's son, Tom, whom she said should have come to collect it.

It was a wonderful family get-together, which continued during the next sitting when Aunt Mary and Tom were our guest sitters. We felt that these sittings exemplified what we had agreed as the purpose of our Saturday Night Club - a regular meeting of friends and relatives from 'both worlds'.

4th October 1947 (73)

This sitting was of great personal interest to me.

My forenames are Thomas William. Thomas is a family name of long standing, but my father also gave me the William. He told me that while he was serving at

Ypres during the 'Great War' he had become like a father to a young 17 year old soldier called Billy Earle who was sadly killed during one of the skirmishes. Dad had felt so close to him he wanted to remember him by giving me the name of William. I never envisaged that I would ever meet my namesake, but along with another soldier pal of Dad's, Jack Seaton, Billy spoke to us, through the trumpet, this night.

The particularly evidential aspect was that Billy called my Dad "Fatha" as he had always done in France. From this evening onwards I was able to relate closely to 'William', and often think of him.

18th October 1947 (75).

It had previously been arranged for Jim McKenzie to take the first of our photographs with his plate camera. This was very much an experiment using the red light set up in the room. He took one each of the ectoplasmic forms of Granny Lumsden and Aunt Agg. Granny stood by the side of the curtain for about four or five minutes. Aunt Agg sat on the vacant chair in front of the curtain and stayed talking to us for about eight minutes.

In the early days of our sittings we had had numerous Spirit lights about the size of shilling, but on the 22nd November (Sitting 80), Douglas brought us something quite different while we had the usual red light on for the materialisations. Quite unexpectedly there was an intense bright flash of light from behind the cabinet curtain, followed by three or four more at short intervals. The light was so bright coming over the top of the curtain, which was level with the picture rail, it lit up the whole room. Because the light was created by our Spirit helpers, it had no ill effect on the medium or the ectoplasm - whereas an ordinary bright torchlight would have had serious ill effects.

Douglas did his 'party trick' for the next three weeks - very exciting and uplifting, but during Sitting 84 he went a step further and lit up Aunt Agg's face just as she stepped out of the cabinet. We hoped he might have been able to develop and extend this form of lighting for other ectoplasmic forms, but unfortunately it did not happen regularly, although he did light up Granny's face during Sitting 90.

Tonight we got our answer about the 'Crusader' badge, which came as an apport two years ago. It belonged to a boy whose mother is a good medium and has seen the Knight Crusader twice in her home. She was able to confirm this. Excellent evidence.

3rd Jan. 1948 (89)

Our first Christmas Party sitting. The details are in the chapter entitled 'Christmas Parties'.

10th Jan. (90)

Another very special night recorded in Chapter 17 'The Homeward Road'

24th Jan. (92),

Mr Jones brought his plate camera to take two more photographs. The camera was set up pointing towards the end of the fireplace at the edge of the cabinet curtain where the materialised forms usually stood.

Granny Lumsden materialised first and stood still for a 90 seconds exposure in a reasonably bright red light and Aunt Agg for about a two-minute exposure. When they were developed the one of Granny was perfectly clear but Aunt Agg must have moved slightly. Before Aunt Agg came Granddad Bessant built and said he was practising for his photo to be taken another time. He stayed about 3 or 4 minutes.

7th February (94),

Terry Abbott, Aunt Agg's youngest son, brought his camera using super-fast film, to take photographs of the materialised forms of Granddad Bessant and then of his own mother who stayed for several minutes to chat with him. Terry was in no doubt that it was his own mother standing in front of him. His father Bob Abbott also built only for a minute, but said he was getting stronger.

As Terry had not used the whole roll of film he returned on 21st Feb. to take his mother again and some group photographs of us all, for record purposes - all with excellent results.

We had now been sitting for almost two years and had enjoyed a tremendous range of physical phenomena, but with the gradual deterioration of my mother's health through cancer, we thought it would be a good idea when we had no guest sitters, to have regular sittings devoted to the mediumship development of other members of the SNC with my mother acting as the Circle leader. The first of these sittings was held on 17th March and two weeks later there were signs of light trance development with Doris and myself. My last recorded notes were made on 3rd April 1948, but I remember that our development was extremely slow and haphazard, and we had no encouraging signs of physical mediumship like my mother.

We continued to have our weekly sittings at Syd and Gladys' home for the next four years until they moved in August 1952. The sittings were then held in our home in Oxford Road. We still enjoyed the trumpet voices and ectoplasmic materialisations as before, but because of the diminishing energy not so many Spirit people were able to come.

During all these sittings as I have already said my mother was receiving much healing energy.

For a number of years during the 1950's we also had a healing Circle in Oxford Road where we were able to help many people in need, the same as my present wife, Ann and I have been doing since we met in 1993. Never forget that the Spirit World needs as many channels as possible for various reasons and purposes - be ready to accept and respond to their overtures, however and whenever they come knocking at your door. You will be richly rewarded!

The Photographs

All the photographs of the Spirit people who materialised were taken primarily for the benefit of my mother who was always in complete trance when the ectoplasm was being taken from her. She never saw any of the ectoplasmic Spirit people who materialised each week nor was she aware of the trumpet movement and the ectoplasm and we hoped that our experimental photographic efforts may produce results which we could all enjoy. We were delighted when we achieved such splendid results as far as we were concerned. I hope you will enjoy them but appreciate they were all simple everyday amateurish 'hit or miss' efforts and not up to 'scientific research' levels.

1. Aunt Agg in her garden in London shortly before her passing in Nov. 1942
2. Granny Lumsden at her front door shortly before she passed over in 1930. (compare it with the spirit face in 4)
3. One of our first efforts on 18th Oct.1947 with a dim red light – Agnes Abbott (Aunt Agg) sitting on a chair, talking to us for some eight minutes. Plate exposure was 2 minutes, hence the head movement as she talked.
4. Granny Lumsden taken on 24th Jan.1948 with Mr Brittain Jones plate camera - on an exposure of 90 seconds
5. Aunt Agg taken on 24th Jan 1948, with a brighter red light – exposure of 2 minutes. The focusing must have been slightly out.
6. Granddad Bessant taken on 7th Feb'48. Because of the red light the beard, which is also ectoplasm looks very dark and quite false but I can assure you it was part of him.
7. Aunt Agg taken on 21st Feb 1948 with a bright red light – exposure 2 minutes with a super-fast film. Note behind Aunt Agg the black curtain, behind which my other was sitting in deep trance. On the left is my father who had obviously moved during the exposure.

1.Aunt Agg in her garden 1942

2. Granny Lumsden 1930

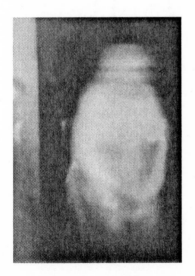

3. Our first attempt, Aunt Agg
materialised, sitting

4. Granny Lumsden
materialised

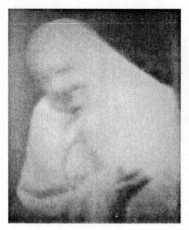 

5.Aunt Agg, materialised
our second attempt

6. Ectoplasmic Materialisation
of my Granddad - with beard

7.Aunt Agg and Tosher taken by Aunt Agg's son, Terry

We had to wait 10 months more before the necessary protection of my mother could be built up against the effects of a 'flash' for infrared pictures. Even then we were told she would feel as though she had been punched in the stomach when she came out of trance. Mr. Brittain Jones provided the infrared equipment and the remaining two photographs were taken in December 1948. The plates, for 'Scientific purposes' were placed in Mr Brittain Jones' plate camera, and exposed in complete darkness by means of a Sashalight bulb enclosed in a light-proof box, made by Sydney, with a Ruby-red Wratten filter set into the front cover (which is in my memorabilia) – rather archaic by today's standards but the results delighted us. As these were taken in complete darkness and the deep ruby red flash through the filter was for a split second only, we saw nothing of the ectoplasm or the trumpet at the time of exposure – as opposed to the earlier photographs, taken in the red light where we saw the ectoplasmic Spirit people while they were being photographed. (A 'Sashalight' was the forerunner of a flashgun and used primarily in portrait photography. It was a large bulb filled with silver paper to increase the output of light.). I had the battery and made the connection to fire the flashgun and expose the plate.

8. Ectoplasm emanating from the medium's mouth.
My mother is sitting in the cabinet corner with the black curtain rolled up. For materialisation purposes the curtain would be hanging to the floor and the Spirit people would use the ectoplasm behind the curtain to 'build' their bodies and then step out into the red light in the room.

9. Shows how the trumpet, by means of an ectoplasmic rod is operated by the Spirit helpers. My mother is again in deep trance, completely unaware of what is happening. Note the shadow of the aluminium trumpet and the solid ectoplasmic rod on the tiled fireplace.

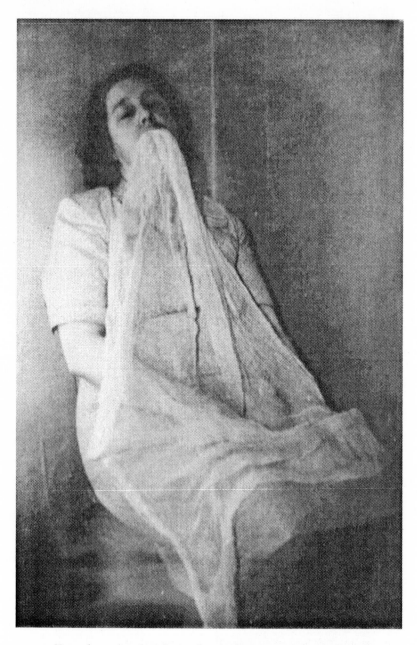

8. Ectoplasm issuing from the medium's mouth. (Infrared)

9. The trumpet supported on an ectoplasmic rod. (Infrared)

A Missed Opportunity

Dr. J. B. Rhine - renowned USA psychologist, was on a UK visit in the late 1940's and was staying in the Middlesbrough area. A good friend of Sydney's, Mr Waddington, was Dr. Rhine's agent at that time and arrangements were made for Mr Brittain Jones and Mr W. W. Fletcher, Headmaster of Middlesbrough High School to meet Dr. Rhine and tell him about our Circle.

Mr Fletcher had been a guest sitter and was so impressed that on the Monday after his sitting he had all the Sixth Form pupils in his study to relate what he had experienced. We learned this from another good friend of Sydney's, Ernie Lowe, a local builder, whose son was one of the pupils. Mr and Mrs Lowe had also been guest sitters on 5th July 1947, Sitting 62, so knew what Mr Fletcher was talking about.

The meeting with Dr. Rhine was on a Wednesday and he was due to sail back to USA at the weekend on the Queen Mary. After a number of telephone calls between us, my mother agreed to sit on the Friday evening, the only evening available to us all, including Mr Fletcher. We had understood this would be suitable for Dr. Rhine, only to be told that he had a meeting in Glasgow that evening - so he never attended the Circle.

It was very interesting to hear later from Mr Waddington that Dr. Rhine had told him that if he could have believed what Mr Jones and Mr Fletcher had told him, he would have postponed his return sailing! It was very difficult to understand his outlook when the information had been given to him by two of the most reputable and highly regarded professional men in the area. We felt he had wasted a unique opportunity to witness at first hand such rare phenomena, which interested him.

13

Alfred (Dad) Kitson

Alfred Kitson, a native of Gawthorpe in West Yorkshire, was one of Spiritualism's early pioneers from the mid-1880's. Throughout the National Union he was affectionately known as 'Dad' Kitson - a true father figure, particularly in the north of England. With his daughter Nellie, another staunch worker for the Movement, he had visited Middlesbrough Church on a few occasions. As a boy I vaguely remembered him - especially his white beard, but Sydney, my mother and father and Doris's parents as church workers, all knew him quite well. So Sitting 47 on 22nd March 1947 proved to be a very special occasion.

Our guests that evening happened to be Doris's parents, Mam and Dad Hudson, whom Sunrise invited quite often because they added much power to the Circle environment. We had been having a red light for the materialisations for three months, but tonight we were experimenting with a rheostat/dimmer made by one of Sydney's friends. This allowed us to control the intensity of the light depending on the experience of the Spirit forms, and proved extremely useful over the years ahead.

The sitting started as usual with the trumpet phenomena and May and Ivy, two of the Hudson family, both spoke to their parents. Sunrise then said it was time for materialisation, so mother moved back into the cabinet in the corner by the fireplace, and within a few minutes he announced our first visitor as "a gentleman - Dad Kitson" -

a very pleasant surprise for us, but we had no idea *how* pleasant it was going to prove.

He built extremely well, complete with beard and stood erect. We could all see him quite clearly in the brighter red light and he stayed for about four minutes. He said he was very pleased to be with us and encouraged us to go on with his work for the Truth of Spiritualism, but he had come that night for a very special reason. Today, he said, was a significant occasion, in that, *exactly* 23 years ago on Saturday 22ⁿᵈ March 1924 he had been honoured to open officially the new Middlesbrough church, at which event Mam and Dad Hudson were church officers. We were all delighted to feel his strong grip when we shook hands with him, especially Mam and Dad Hudson, who said they would have to check the church records for the opening date - they certainly could not remember after so many years. But Dad Kitson *could* remember and needless to say he was proved absolutely correct! As another piece of evidence he gave his birth date as 15ᵗʰ February 1855, which none of us knew - and again he was proved correct when we checked in his autobiography. He told us that his daughter Nellie had accompanied him and she was also pleased to be with us.

As you will have gathered, this had been a very special and unique sitting, so I sent a report to Ernest Thompson, the editor of the journal, 'Two Worlds', which he published on 25ᵗʰ April. Two months later I received a letter, still in my possession, dated 25ᵗʰ June, from George Mack who lived near Warrington in which he wrote:

"I was very interested in the record of the séance you held in Middlesbrough in which you report Dad Kitson materialised. I know that Dad was very interested in Middlesbrough and it is probably one of the places he would try to contact after his passing.

"There have been so many reports of him manifesting at different places, of some of which I have very grave doubts. This has caused me to make enquiries for details of séances in order that I might try to confirm his presence at those séances. May I say that I was counted one of the intimate friends of Dad Kitson. He was one of the privileged persons, which could be counted on one hand, who sat in our Home Circle whenever he paid visits to our house. Well! He and I made a pact, which is not known to others, so that when he returns I can confirm his identity. I am in touch with him through our own Circle and he manifests through trance control but always gives and confirms the secret signs.

"Could I prevail upon you sometime, if it is not putting you to too much inconvenience, to let me know of any other séances that you hold at which he manifests. I make this request as much in your interest as mine. I wish your Circle every success. It is marvellous what can be done with harmonious, constant, regular and self-sacrificing sittings. Yours, very sincerely, Geo. A. Mack."

We were very pleased and interested to receive Mr Mack's letter and agreed we would try to help him should Dad Kitson manifest again. As he said, it was as much for our benefit as for his, and although he did not actually manifest again, we had a message via Sunrise at Sitting 63 on 12th July 1947. At the very end of the sitting after the materialisations had finished, Sunrise spoke to us and said "Alfred Kitson is here and gives this message - 'Right hand symbol of Goodwill, Left hand symbol of Fraternal Love'."

I immediately wrote to George Mack and was thrilled to receive his confirmation that this was their secret sign.

I feel sure you will agree that we could not have had more conclusive proof of the visit that night, the 22nd March 1947, of Alfred 'Dad' Kitson because we received the following information:

1) Two dates which none of us in the room was aware off, thus no 'mind reading' accusation.

2) A secret sign known only to the two intimate friends.

As I have said so often, our Spirit friends never forget us and frequently jog our memories if we tend to forget

132

them. Many thanks, 'Dad' and Nellie, for your thoughtful and memorable return visit to Middlesbrough.

Saying a Prayer

There's never a night goes by
but someone's saying a prayer
That the one they dearly love
will be helped their pain to bear;
That the morning will bring strength
and hope dispel all fears;
This prayer is being said tonight
by a thousand hearts in tears.

There's never a morning breaks
but some of our hopes come true;
Maybe it's turned out this way
for the one you love – and you.
But remember those still weeping
and whose prayers have seemed in vain –
Then out of your thankful heart
say the prayer you prayed – again.

M.R.H.

14

First anniversary - Sunrise materialises

26ᵗʰ April 1947 – Sitting No. 52

Sunrise had especially asked for Mam and Dad Hudson to be guests on this night as he had promised to try to materialise and needed the extra power; otherwise we were the usual eight. We started 15 minutes earlier and the feeling of the power in the room was quite strong. The first speaker through the trumpet was, Mrs Puckrin, an old Middlesbrough church member, who spoke quite clearly. Sunrise then spoke and said the conditions were very good indeed. Sam Hildred then came for his usual chat, quite clear and instructive, and said he had brought some flowers for Mrs Hildred for their Wedding Anniversary.

We found them on the hearth at the end of the sitting - five lovely carnations. We asked him whether he could find out if it was the flowers that were de-materialised or part of the wall, to bring them through. He said he would try to let us know later. He had a long chat and stayed nine minutes - not easy through the trumpet. Sunrise then suggested we moved on to materialisation, so my mother moved back into the cabinet and we switched on the red light.

The first materialisation was Mr Brittain Jones' Spirit guide called Ali Bey Ahtum, but he was unable to stay long. At least Mr Jones had the opportunity to meet him. Dad Hudson's Uncle Tom then built up, well formed with beard. He spoke clearly but could not stay long, which is not unusual for those building for the first time. The normal practice was for Sunrise to take over between materialisations and introduce the next visitor, but tonight was different. As soon as Tom Hudson had gone we heard a voice in the cabinet calling "Annie, Annie,", Mam Hudson's Christian name. Annie responded and her mother, Granny Lumsden, immediately walked out of the cabinet. They were both delighted to meet again.

During a previous sitting, Sunrise said that when he built he would try to bring us one of his feathers as well as an ectoplasmic one, so we had been asked to put on the mantelpiece a small jar with about half an inch of water in the bottom. To be sure, in case of accidents, Gladys put two medium-sized Sandwich Spread jars, each with half an inch of water and the lids separately on the mantelpiece.

Then came what we had been eagerly looking forward to for many months - Sunrise announced, quite simply - "We will build." Before he came however, he told us not to leave our seats and we would not be able to shake hands, as the control would not be as strong as usual, which we fully understood. He had obviously examined the jars on the mantelpiece and told us there was not quite enough water in them but not to worry they would see to it!

He then materialised, quite tall, in his ectoplasmic robes, complete with feathered head-dress and stood for a minute or two just in front of the cabinet curtain, in full view in the red light - a most imposing figure who had become a very close friend and protector during the 12 months of our sittings. A wonderful moment for all of us, and before he went he told us 'the lady' would follow with the two feathers.

Aunt Agg, known to Sunrise as 'the lady', immediately followed, holding a feather in each hand. One was an apported ordinary orange coloured feather, which she placed on the mantelpiece and is now part of my treasured memorabilia. The other was a white ectoplasmic feather, which she handed to my father to be passed round the sitters. We were all naturally very excited about this, so much so that about halfway round it was dropped on the floor. I immediately got on to my knees to retrieve it and let it continue its journey, which ended with me. It felt like a quill feather, not downy, quite stiff but flexible - nothing like the apported feather which we examined later.

After I had examined it I passed it back to Doris, sitting alongside me, to hand back to Aunt Agg who had quietly been standing in the room witnessing our excitement. Instead of taking the feather she asked Doris to put it in the jar which Aunt Agg had just picked up from the mantelpiece, after which she picked up the lid and we were all intrigued to watch her screwing the lid on the jar containing the ectoplasmic feather.

Apart from bringing the feathers, Aunt Agg stayed for about nine minutes and had a good chat. She was very pleased that we had all, in both worlds, had such an enjoyable year together and said *they* were quite astounded by the progress that had been made. We replied that we were equally astounded, but it was all their work and we were only too happy to provide the necessary conditions. After Aunt Agg had gone, Uncle Jack just popped his head round the cabinet curtain to say, "How do everybody" and was gone!

Sunrise closed by asking us always to remember the original intention of the Saturday Night Club - to keep a regular date and meeting with old friends and relatives from the Spirit World. When we were 'experimenting' it was difficult for them to come and although he wanted us to continue with the scientific side, he did not want us to become too absorbed and forget 'our pals'. He assured Mr Jones he would still be able to cut off a piece of Aunt Agg's robes in the future - Mr Jones was keen to examine it. An excellent and amazing sitting of one and a half hours, which closed at 9.20 pm. A real Anniversary celebration!

On examination after the sitting it was seen that there was at least twice as much liquid in the jar containing the feather, at least an inch, but none had been taken from the other jar. There was no sign of fluid elsewhere. We all had a good look at the ectoplasmic feather using Sydney's watch repairing magnifying glass, with my mother being particularly interested of course.

It had felt rather like plastic and also looked like it under the glass. Sunrise had told us it would soon disappear and in fact we were able to witness that as we sat having supper. The part above the fluid level seemed gradually to melt away into droplets and run into the bottom of the jar. The feather was put into the jar at about 9 pm. and by 11.30 pm. it had completely disappeared leaving only the yellowish fluid. We removed the lid to smell the contents, which gave off an acrid bleach-like odour, not unlike the odour for the first few minutes when the Spirits materialise in their ectoplasmic form.

At the end of the following week's sitting (53) Sunrise passed on the apologies of the Spirit chemist (called Swift) for the 'queer' smell with the feather last week. He explained that the stalk was an ordinary apport to support the ectoplasmic plumage, and the liquid he had added to the jar helped to preserve the ectoplasm but destroyed the apported stalk. We all had a bit of a chuckle to think about the Spirit chemist apologising to us after the remarkable work he had carried out. We asked Sunrise to pass on our sincere thanks for his great efforts. A truly harmonious, loving and trustworthy relationship had indeed developed between the two worlds, and so it continued for the many years ahead.

15

Jack Graham

I got to know Jack during 1947 when he had a fish and chip shop at the other end of Garnet Street from where Mam and I had our shop. When I had finished my preparation work I used to go along to help Jack, whose opening hours did not clash with ours. We put the world to right as we sat on upturned fish boxes working and soon got to discussing life after death and our remarkable Home Circle.

Jack had been brought up as a member of the Plymouth Brethren who apparently believe there is nothing after we die. As he would put it - when we're dead we're done for. He was a very perceptive young man and by the time he reached his twenties he began to question their beliefs and looked around elsewhere, but was never satisfied with what he heard. There must be something else he thought.

Our Home Circle at Syd and Gladys Shipman's home, with trumpet voices and full ectoplasmic spirit materialisations, was sitting every Saturday night and we had reached the stage where we had permission from our Spirit helpers to invite guests. I had told Jack about our wonderful experiences and he became intensely interested and asked if he could be on the waiting list of potential guests. I told him it could be many months ahead, even a year or so, which he fully accepted but just hoped it could be sooner - and so it came to pass...another of those 'fancy that' occurrences with an unexpected ending.

Shortly after Jack's name had been put on the list, Syd rang me one Saturday morning to say that the lady who was to have been our guest that evening was unable to attend, and was there anyone else who could come at such short notice. I immediately thought of Jack and went to his shop at once. Although he was due in the shop that night he excitedly accepted and said he would definitely arrange for his son Albert to take his place, irrespective of Albert's previous arrangements - and so he did. No way was he going to miss such a unique opportunity.

As always, we started in the dark as advised by our Spirit helpers, and a number of Spirit people came and spoke through the 'trumpet'. After about 20 minutes the trumpet phenomena was brought to an end by Sunrise and we switched on the red light for the materialisation phenomena and we had quite a number of ectoplasmic Spirit materialisations that night.

Jack's Aunt Edna came and talked to him about old times when "we used to play together" which naturally pleased him no end, and after the sitting had finished we talked over supper until after 11 pm. Jack was clearly so impressed by what had happened that night and was so excited that he personally, on that very special Saturday night, had witnessed many materialised spirit people walking around the room, talking to us, in red light. He went home with a completely different outlook about life after death. He had at last found what he had been seeking for so many years.

About 10 am the following morning I had a telephone call from his son Albert, who had taken over in the shop on the previous evening, to tell me what had happened when his Dad got home about midnight - long past his usual bedtime. Jack had immediately gone upstairs and roused his two sons and his daughter with the order to get downstairs and listen to what he had to tell them. Jack was generally a quiet man but when in that mood nobody dare oppose him - so down they all went and sat on the settee.

Apparently Jack spoke very strongly with great emphasis: "Sit there - listen to what I have to tell you - it is all true and never forget it!" He continued for over an hour describing in great detail all the remarkable phenomena he had witnessed. Albert found it very hard to believe and was really ringing me to get confirmation that his Dad was not making it all up, although he realised that that was most unlikely from such a down-to-earth man as Jack talking to his family.

Exactly a week later on the next Sunday morning, I had another call from Albert with a quite different message. He was ringing to tell me that his father had passed away during the night, just one week after his unexpected visit to our Home Circle! It would appear that Jack had *had* to come to the Circle the previous Saturday to find what he had been seeking, and which prepared him for his unexpected transition to the Spirit World.

Within five weeks of his passing, being the strong character he was, and no doubt still is, he spoke to us through the trumpet. He thanked us for what we had done for him, which enabled him to understand what had happened when he passed over. He continued to come and speak to us quite often and regularly repeated his thanks.

During our chats in his fish shop he had mentioned an old Plymouth Brethren friend, a Mr Matheson, who turned out to be a neighbour of ours in Lambeth Road. Mr Matheson had apparently remained a member of the Plymouth Brethren and lived with his two spinster daughters two doors from Doris and me. Sometime after Jack had passed over, Mr Matheson collapsed at the nearby bus stop and passed over through a heart attack.

The first time Jack spoke to us after Mr Matheson's passing I asked him if he had perhaps been able to contact Mr M. "Oh yes, he replied - but we have a problem. He does not believe he is dead!" His belief that there was nothing after life on earth was so strong that he was sure he was still on the earth. Apparently he used to return to his home and talk to his daughters who ignored him! This made him extremely frustrated and he just could not understand it.

No doubt this is just how some Poltergeists feel before losing their self-control and using the latent energy to move material objects - just to attract attention. Fortunately Mr Matheson, a mature man in his sixties, must have retained his self-control and as far as we knew, no such phenomena occurred in his home.

Jack tried to explain things to him but his only comment was that he could not possibly be dead otherwise there would just be nothing and he would not be able to speak to Jack.

The fact that Jack explained that he also was dead had no immediate effect. Obviously Jack never gave up, because many months later when he came to speak to us he was delighted to be able to report that he had eventually made him understand and Mr Matheson was now feeling much more relaxed. If only everyone was aware of this great Truth - that we simply continue to live, but on a higher vibration - as Jack Graham had discovered just that vital week before his passing.

~~~~

"And ever near us though unseen,
Our Dear Immortal Spirits tread'
For all the Boundless Universe is life –
There are no dead."

16

Roy Dixon Smith

The Saturday Night Club had been sitting for over two years when Sydney saw a letter in his copy of 'Psychic News', a weekly Spiritualist journal, from Roy Dixon Smith who lived in London. He said he was investigating Spiritualism and was especially interested, along with many hundreds of others, in "experiencing genuine materialisation." As the safety of my mother, our medium, was of paramount importance at all times, all our guest sitters so far, were either known to us personally or vouched for by reliable contacts, as being genuine, trustworthy people.

Roy Dixon Smith did not fit into either category - but Sydney felt strongly enough to bring his letter to our attention. After seriously discussing it we all felt as strongly as Sydney, so decided to go ahead and offer him the opportunity to sit with us. Most importantly my mother was in full agreement, but if there had been the slightest doubt in her mind, the invitation would never have been sent. She was quite sure our Spirit friends were guiding us in the right direction.

He was a complete stranger to all of us, as you will gather from his writing, but I have since summarized the following brief biographical information from his book 'New Light on Survival', published in 1952. A Lt. Colonel in the Indian Army, he was a man of some standing.

While serving in India in 1934 he met Betty and her husband Stuart. After hearing of Stuart's death in 1937, he made contact with Betty and they were married in 1939.

Their life together was very brief as Betty died of a heart disease in 1944. Then began his determined quest for evidence of Survival beyond death, through Spiritualism. Having retired from the Army, he contacted the Marylebone Spiritualist Association (later to become The Spiritualist Association of Great Britain) in London in 1945. There he was given impressive evidence through a psychometry reading, including the names of Betty and Ethel - which was Betty's real name but was never used. From then on he travelled far and wide in his search and sat with many well-known mediums, but had never witnessed ectoplasmic materialization. Hence his letter in the 'Psychic News'. He was so impressed with the evidence he received in our Circle that he included his experiences in his book, as follows: -

"On the afternoon of 9th October (1948) I was met at the station by Mr Shipman. He took me in his car to his home where I found that a bedroom had been placed at my disposal, and I was entertained freely and most hospitably for the weekend.

They knew nothing whatever about me and had never heard of me (and vice-versa) until after my letter had appeared in the paper. The house was of the same general type as the one at Buckie, my host and his friends likewise business and professional people of the same outlook and social background. The circle whom I met that evening consisted of Mr and Mrs Shipman, the parents of Mrs Shipman*, Mrs Harrison the medium, who is an intimate friend of the Shipmans' and a short and somewhat plump middle-aged lady bearing not the least resemblance to Betty, her son and daughter-in-law, and a well-known local doctor. I mention all these details to show how utterly preposterous and ridiculous would be any suggestion of fraud, even had it been possible to produce thereby the results described.

My letter in the 'Psychic News' said that I wanted these experiences to include in a book, and thus that anyone who might give them to me would, in a way, probably be rendering a public service; and that is why they answered my plea, but they insisted, quite naturally, on my not disclosing their address to avoid being pestered by curiosity-mongers and others. For evidential reasons I revealed no details of my private life before the séance was over, and for the same reason they would have refused to have listened to them, since they were just as anxious as I for genuine evidence.

The room in which the séance was held is much the same as the one at Buckie[1] except that there is only one door, that being in the same relative position to the cabinet and sitters as the window is in the Buckie house, while the mantelpiece is alongside and on the right of the corner that contained the cabinet. The cabinet in this case consisted of a single black curtain, which I helped to hang up myself across the corner of the room; it enclosed a space barely big enough to hold the medium on her chair.

The light during the séance was a bright red electric light bulb in a bowl suspended from the centre of the ceiling. The room throughout the materializations was thus brightly illuminated and the forms and their faces clearly seen. The circle of chairs was arranged close up to and blocking the door, and thus a little farther from the cabinet than at Buckie. The door was locked and the séance then commenced.

The first phase was 'direct voice' in the dark through a luminous-banded trumpet (better called megaphone) which darted about the room, sometimes high in the air, and often accompanying the singing like a conductor's baton. The trumpet hovered in front of the sitter to be addressed, and the voices came through, all being quite loud but some difficult to understand while others are perfectly clear. The circle guide, speaking through the trumpet, then gave an excellent description of Betty, remarking on her height, slimness, and beauty; all being facts unknown to anyone present except myself. Betty then attempted to speak to me; after prolonged and seemingly painful effort and a few exclamations to the effect that she couldn't do it, she managed to say, "I am your Betty".

During this phase, large pink carnations were apported into the room, one being dropped on each sitter's lap including mine. They were quite fresh. and moist as if with dew. There were no flowers of this type previously in the room or, so my host told me, anywhere else in the house. The medium all the while had been sitting with the rest of us in the circle and was not in trance.

At the close of this phase, which seemed to me to last about a quarter of an hour, the red light was switched on, the medium took her seat behind the curtain, and the materializations commenced, of which there were about half a dozen in all.

I was introduced to each one of them in turn; all being deceased friends and close relatives of the sitters and thus thoroughly well known to them. I rose from my chair, walked up to them and shook them by the hand, and we made conventional remarks to each other just exactly as everyone does when first meeting a stranger. They were swathed in white muslin-like draperies and cowls that were the exact replicas of those worn by the forms in the Buckie séance.

They were solid, natural and, except for their apparel, exactly like ordinary living people. In fact, had everyone been dressed similarly, it would have been quite impossible to distinguish these materialized forms from the rest of the company. Their hands felt perfectly natural and life-like in every respect and their handgrips were very firm. They smiled, laughed, and chatted to me and the others; all their features, complexions, and expressions being perfectly clear in that ample light.

I repeat (and surely I cannot be more explicit) they were exactly like you or me in muslin draperies, and they behaved as we would behave if we dropped in amongst a circle of friends and relations plus one stranger for a few minutes' visit, and they were welcomed accordingly and just as naturally and unemotionally as we would be. There were mutual cheery goodbyes as they departed, sinking apparently through the floor in precisely the same manner as the forms at Buckie.

My introduction to the first of them was 'Come and meet Aunt Gladys'*, the sister of the medium, and she was most charming and vivacious as she offered me her hand and smiled and chatted to me. Then came 'Grannie', and as I was presented to her the doctor said to me 'Feel her pulse'. The old lady chuckled, extended her arm, made some humorous remark about 'mucking her about' or something to that effect, and I pressed my fingers into her wrist. All the sinews were there and the wrist felt and looked absolutely natural; the beat of the pulse was strong and regular.

'Now feel her feet,' said the doctor, and I bent down and felt the foot that the laughing old lady extended from her long draperies. It felt rather spongy or woolly and was apparently about to dissolve, for just after that the old lady bade us farewell and vanished. Then came a man with a twisted face drawn down rather grotesquely on the right side, as a consequence of which he could only mumble incoherently. I was introduced to him by name, and as I shook his hand my host explained, 'He always comes like this. He died of a stroke.'

I cannot remember the next two or three visitors very clearly, but what I have said of the others applies equally to them; and by then the slight feeling of oddity at this amazing experience had left me, for it was all so absolutely natural. They all differed drastically in face, figure, voice, and mannerism, and in every case their eyes were open; while, of course, the movements of their features as they laughed and talked by itself disposes of the suggestion of a set of masks, should the most unreasonable of sceptics have such an idea in mind, and should he also have such a strange opinion of human nature as to imagine that anyone would lavish free hospitality on a stranger for the sole satisfaction of tricking him.

The guide then announced the coming of Betty and asked us to sing one of her favourite songs. We sang 'I'll Walk Beside You', in the middle of which a tall slim figure emerged from the curtain and stood silently in view.

I rose from my chair and walked up to the figure, taking the extended hand in mine. I examined the hand, and it was just like Betty's and quite unlike the medium's. I stared into the face, and recognized my wife. We spoke to each other, though what we said I cannot remember, for I was deeply stirred and so was she and her voice was incoherent with emotion.

'Can he kiss you?' someone asked, and Betty murmured, 'Yes'. I then kissed her on the lips, which were warm, soft, and natural. Thereupon she bent her head and commenced to weep, and in a moment or two she sank. I watched her form right down to the level the floor at my feet where it dissolved, the last wisp of it being drawn within the cabinet.

After I had resumed my seat, there was a pause, perhaps to allow me to recover some of my lost composure; and then the circle guide announced another visitor for me, giving the name 'John Fletcher', and saying that he was a clergyman who had been helping to inspire my book - perhaps the 'clergyman guide' referred to by the male medium in Chapter III, but of whose authenticity I was distinctly dubious.

A tall black-bearded figure then appeared, and when I reached him he gave my hand a very powerful hearty grip, expressed his delight at this meeting between us and my realization, at last, of his own reality, discussed the book with me, declared that the work was now complete, bade me a cordial farewell, and vanished in the usual manner.

If I once doubted the existence of guides, how can I do so now?

I have told my tale baldly, without any dramatizing or sentimental frills; it must surely be a pathetically warped mind, which cannot supply such omissions from its own imagination." (end of quote)

* There are a couple of mistaken identities in this extract. Because we were introduced to him *en masse* just minutes before the sitting started, my father was mistakenly remembered as one of Mrs Shipman's parents, whereas only her mother, Mrs Hildred was present and her father, Sam Hildred, was a regular communicator from the Spirit World.

'Aunt Gladys' should, of course, be 'Aunt Agg' our main communicator. Gladys is Mrs Shipman's first name.

[1] 'Buckie' is the name of a town in Scotland where he had previously had a sitting with a Mrs D.

~~~~

Looking forward !

Take the road that stretches out before you,
Walk in the dusk and know the end is bright.
Take what comes and find the way to glory,
Much may go wrong – but even more comes right.

Face the day however hard before you
And with the tears upon your cheek still wet,
Learn to smile and keep on looking forward –
Life is not done because the Sun is set.

M.R.H.

17

The Homeward Road

During our Children's Christmas party sitting (89) on the 3rd January 1948, a young man spoke quietly through the trumpet. He gave his name as Andrew, had lived at Haverton Hill, had died in 1941, but could not remember much else. He promised to come again with more information.

He kept his promise the following Saturday, during which sitting he again spoke through the trumpet and by a series of questions and answers he told us his name was James Andrew Fleming, had passed over when he was about 12 years old on 6th June 1941, had no brothers or sisters but did have a pet dog of which he was very fond.

He had been attracted to our Circle by the bright light emanating from it. He was still a bit unsure, he said, but thought he had lived in Coniston Avenue, or something like that in Haverton Hill. He had tried to visit his home, he said, but there seemed to be a mist, which he could not get through. Was it near us and could we help him?

Haverton Hill was a village, near Middlesbrough, built to accommodate the workers at the vast Imperial Chemical Industries factory at Billingham. I was free the following Wednesday afternoon and told him I would go there to see if I could find his home, and invited him to accompany me - with the help of perhaps Aunt Agg or other Spirit people familiar to him. We would try to penetrate that misty barrier and link him again with his mother and father - and his pet dog, if still there.

Not knowing Haverton Hill at all well, I stopped my car at the local butcher's shop. Did they know a Coniston Avenue? No, sorry - but there is a Collinson Road just around the corner. I thanked them and drove round. Facing me was a long road of council houses, four or five to a block, with small front gardens - similar to the thousands built in the 1930's. There was I, at three o'clock on a very cold Wednesday afternoon - not a soul in sight. I sat wondering where to start my enquiries - which were unusual to say the least. 'Collinson'.... 'Coniston'.... they were very similar, so I *must* have a try, for James's sake, and I had promised him I would, but which door do I knock on? The answer was quickly presented to me when I saw a lady coming out another house about three blocks away.

I immediately jumped out of the car and approached her mustering as much confidence as I could: "Excuse me, but could you perhaps tell me where the Flemings live, please?" Imagine my amazement when she promptly replied "Oh yes, just on the corner there at No.20." Could it possibly be as easy as this I thought?

I walked over and rang the bell at No.20. No reply. I rang again. Still no reply, but a woman appeared at the door of the adjoining house. Could she help perhaps? Helpful 'nosey' neighbours were the forerunners of today's 'Neighourhood Watch' schemes! "Yes please," I replied, "I was wanting to speak to Mrs Fleming."

The wife/mother automatically came to my mind as I thought she was more likely to be at home at that time of the day. The husband would no doubt be still at work.

"No," she said, "she is out at present - works at the ICI canteen and won't be home until about 4.30." I thanked her and said I would try to return about 7.30 and perhaps she would mention it to Mrs Fleming when she returned home.

I returned around 7.30 pm. - a pitch black and still extremely cold January night, with very dim gas street lighting, as was usual in those days. Again I rang the bell at No.20 - perhaps more apprehensively this time, wondering what was ahead of me. This time there was a reply, quite quickly in fact, and I was confronted by a very stern looking man.

"Are you the chap who came for my wife this afternoon?" he barked at me before I had time to speak! Oh dear, I thought - what have I done! Is this the home I'm really looking for? "Yes sir," I replied, as friendly as possible, "but I would also like to speak to you if I may."

"Well, what do you want?" he snapped back. As I have said, my enquiries were rather unusual, even without such an opening confrontation. "Ah well," I thought, "here goes - just ask simple questions and play it by ear."

"Did you have a son called James Andrew?" "Yes" came the reply. "Was he about 12 years old when he died?" Back came another curt "Yes." "Did he die on 6th June 1941?" I asked, now feeling quite inwardly excited.

"Yes" he said again, not quite so aggressively this time, but quickly added, "How do you know, and what's this all about?" A very reasonable question to put to a complete stranger who knocks on your door on a dark winter's night.

"I'm researching some information about psychic phenomena and was hoping that you may be able to assist me," I replied. Little did he realise how much he had already done so. Three questions - three affirmatives! All this, still at the front door, in the space of three or four minutes - and I confirmed their name was Fleming.

Had I really found the home of James Andrew, who had spoken to us from the Spirit World, for the first time, only four days previously? It certainly seemed like it - but more was yet to come. By this time a lady had also appeared at the doorway.

"What's happening? What does he want?" she asked apprehensively. Mr Fleming quickly explained but in a much more subdued voice, and without the original aggression. "Well would you like to come in and talk?" said the lady, and I seemed to detect a sense of expectancy in her voice. "Many thanks - it is rather cold tonight out here."

From the moment we entered their living room the atmosphere seemed to change - much friendlier, although still rather apprehensive. A cheerful open fire greeted us and I sat in an armchair next to the sideboard, on which was a. framed photograph of a good-looking boy - surely James, I thought.

Mr and Mrs Fleming sat on the settee on the other side of the fireplace facing me - still a complete stranger asking questions about their dead son. But the friendliness continued. "Would you like a cup of tea?" asked Mrs Fleming. "Many thanks" I replied.

As Mrs Fleming went through to the kitchen, a rough-haired terrier bounded out and immediately sat in front of me with his tail wagging vigorously, ears pricked and whining rather than barking. "Most unusual," remarked Mr Fleming, "he's not usually so friendly with strangers."

But as I explained to them, he wasn't looking directly at me, rather over my right shoulder where no doubt James was standing behind me. Yes, this was James's dog, 'Rags', and he was welcoming him home! I truly felt so pleased that James was back with his parents.

Mission accomplished I thought - and I would be leaving after I had enjoyed my cup of tea. But not so. As Mrs Fleming handed me the cup of tea she rather diffidently said - "We're Catholics, you see," with all the attendant implications. I immediately offered to leave and assured them I had no intention of offending their religious beliefs or principles.

"Oh no," she said, "we would like to talk to you," and her husband nodded in agreement. From then on Mrs Fleming did most of the talking - a mother's natural love for her only child being very evident.

I explained briefly about our small group and how we had heard their son's voice last Saturday evening. They listened intently and with obvious interest. There was certainly no indication of any feeling of disbelief. I felt sure they accepted James was with them.

Although it was a few days past Twelfth Night, I noticed there were still a few Christmas decorations in the room. What was unusual however, was why they were there at all. During our talk, Mrs Fleming told me she had had a strange feeling around Christmas time that she should get a tree and decorate the room as they had always done when James was alive. The feeling was so strong, although she had no idea why, that she unpacked all the decorations, which they had put away and had never used since James died - over six years before. She now realised, she said, why the feeling was so strong this particular year and felt so very pleased that she had done it!

I now felt that my visit had not only been instrumental in getting James back to his home, but equally important, his mother and father were aware of his presence and happily accepted the situation. The 'mist' that James had been unable to penetrate had now been lifted and the Fleming family was again complete. My anticipated brief call had turned into a two hours long, very interesting and satisfying visit.

Another very interesting incident occurred during my visit. In those days, front doors were never locked until the occupants went to bed, so it was no surprise when we heard the front door open and a young lady announced her arrival. I did wonder how they were going to explain my presence under such unusual circumstances, but full credit to Mrs Fleming, Catholic or not, she quietly explained exactly the purpose of my visit to the young lady, whom I gathered from the conversation was also Catholic.

I'm sure Mrs Fleming could never even have thought of, let alone expected, the response she received. In a rather sheepish manner, the young lady quickly told them that now she was so pleased to be able to tell them that she had been going to the local Spiritualist church in Norton for the past six months - but just could not tell them until tonight! So my visit had served two very useful purposes.

James's joy and that of his parents, was matched by ours at being able to help them all in such a positive manner. I did leave an open invitation for the Flemings to come as guest sitters, but unfortunately, as might be expected, we heard nothing from them.

The bright light that James had seen emanating from our Circle on that Saturday evening had been like a beacon to him, and he came to thank us the following Saturday - this time in a much stronger and clearer voice!

That same bright spiritual and psychic light was also a beacon to many other frustrated confused or simply lost Spirits whom we were so pleased to help over the years of our sittings.

I am pleased to say now, that James came back every year during our Christmas party sittings to thank us for our help.

I am sure you will appreciate that this is evidence of Spirit survival of the highest quality, because James came to us that evening as a complete stranger, and none of us knew anything about him or his family. Yet I was able to follow the sketchy information he gave us and prove conclusively that it was 100 per cent accurate.

The overworked excuse/reason so often used by the sceptics, that mediums obtain their information from the sitters' minds without them realising it, just could *not* apply in this case.

I have given this chapter the title of the poem written by my mother, which expresses the feelings of so many like Mr and Mrs Fleming. Numerous people have used it as a reading, during burial services. Many of them were not Spiritualists but appreciated the true meaning of the words.

The Homeward Road

You have passed beyond our sight along the unseen way,
On the homeward journey that we all must take some day.
In heart and home you leave a gap that no one else can fill,
You have gone - and yet it seems that you are near us still.

You're only just a step ahead around the hidden bend -
On the road that leads us homeward to our journey's end.
Though the sorrows of bereavement linger in our mind,
Happy is the memory that you have left behind.

M.R.H.

18

The Christmas Parties

Each year, when mother's health condition allowed, we held during the Christmas period a special Christmas Party sitting for the Spirit children, and I would like to tell you about some of the exciting happenings during two of those sittings. Our first party was on 3ʳᵈ January 1948, and I have my notes about it in front of me. The other held on 5ᵗʰ January 1954 was indeed very special, insofar as the whole one and a half hours was recorded, on a reel-to-reel tape recorder, by our good friend Jim McKenzie. I still treasure my copy of that original recording, but such tapes, unfortunately, are quite ephemeral and after 50 years are likely to lose the clarity of the speech and disintegrate. Fortunately, ours is still in reasonable condition, and thanks to a very friendly and supportive BBC radio producer, we have an even better, permanent copy on a Compact Disc. Our grateful thanks Chris.

As a family with five young children we naturally had a Christmas tree each year which we re-decorated especially for these sittings with small inexpensive toys like rattles, cars, aeroplanes, dolls, ships, strings of beads, baubles etc. and always told the Spirit children they could remove them from the tree, play with them in the room and take away as many as they wanted - if they could manage it.

Needless to say that every year they took us at our word and when the light went on at the end of each sitting, we saw that some of the toys had been removed from the tree and were not in the room. Aunt Agg told us that the children used to remove them from the tree, play with them on the floor and then de-materialise them to take them out of the house. We never knew the exact destination of each toy but were told the Spirit children took them to the areas where very poor, deprived children lived and simply re-materialised them alongside such a child, who was overjoyed to find a new plaything - thus sharing joy and happiness in both worlds!

During the 1948 party we received four tulips and a bunch of violets as apports. Doris's parents, Mam and Dad Hudson, were our guests that night and our good Spirit helper Brownie spoke through the trumpet and said he had been to their home and apported a small pot dog of theirs which we would find later. We found it at the close of the sitting, in the bucket which held the tree, and Mam Hudson was delighted to take it back home as a memory of the party.

Sunrise told us a little African boy wanted to communicate by whistling 'Swanee River' through the trumpet. The tune was very clear and bright and we all joined in by singing quietly - quite a moving moment. Four others spoke through the trumpet, including Sam Hildred, a regular communicator and a young man called Andrew, who passed over when he was 12 years old, but could not remember much more that night. He promised to come again, which he did the following week and gave us much more information, which led to the story I have written in the previous chapter.

Just before my mother moved into the cabinet for the materialisation we had a lovely surprise. We all felt something drop on to our knees, in the dark, which created a lot of excitement and laughter (always beneficial in a Circle). We discovered that Sydney, Dad Hudson, Mr Jones and my father had each got a cigar and the rest of us got some wrapped toffees. As a non-smoker I was pleased to get the toffees of course. Brownie told us he had apported the cigars from a big party for men only in London, and the kiddies had brought the toffees from another big party, also in London.

There were a couple of intriguing and interesting points about these particular apports. Brownie said he had got three of the cigars out of a large box and commented that they would never be missed as there were far too many for the members there, and a lot would probably be wasted. The fourth one, he had obtained, in his own words, "whipped it out of a chap's fingers just as he was about to light it - and he was still looking round for it blaming one of his mates!" When the light went on we found three cigars were wrapped but the fourth one had the end cut off ready to light - confirming Brownie's words. We could just imagine the confusion at the party and had a good laugh about it - typical barrow boy's fun.

However, there was something of greater interest about the toffees. Sydney and Gladys sold confectionery in their shop but were completely puzzled by the make shown on the wrappers. I did not record it but think it was 'Vanity Fair', but it was certainly a make completely unknown in Middlesbrough. I should mention here that confectionery sales in 1948 were still regionalised and strictly rationed.

Sydney was very keen to find out more, so he showed a couple of them to their confectionery sales representative without disclosing their source. Mr D the sales representative was completely unaware of the name and possibly thought they had been brought by some visitors from another area in the UK. He promised to make further enquiries, which eventually revealed that this particular make of sweets was limited for sale in the *London area only*. This was further confirmation of Brownie's words and as we know, distance creates no problems for Spirit apports.

My notes show we had seven materialisations during this party sitting. Firstly: Granny Lumsden, who came to give greetings to her daughter and son-in-law, Mam and Dad Hudson. Granny was followed by May - one of Dad Hudson's daughters by his first wife Hannah; then Hannah herself immediately followed, and stayed quite a while chatting. She lovingly thanked Mam Hudson for looking after the family of five children whom Mam had 'inherited', as a young bride of 23, when she married Dad Hudson.

It was a very emotional and unique family meeting, linking the two worlds, and Hannah rested her face on Dad's shoulder before kissing him as she departed. I can still sense that emotion more than 50 years later.

Charles Roeder, past President of Middlesbrough Church, then 'built', (a term we use for 'materialised') complete with beard, and brought with him a very special apport, which he handed to me personally. It was his own Lyceum lapel badge, with an inset photograph of Andrew Jackson Davis, one of the earliest American pioneers of Spiritualism, which he always wore on his jacket. Where he had found it we never knew but for all the years of our circle it was always pinned to the front of the cabinet curtain and is now another treasured item in my memorabilia. (see photograph of apports)

Two other old Lyceumist friends built, and chatted, Ernie Buckingham and Ronnie Lofthouse, and finally Aunt Agg came for her usual weekly chat of course. During the sitting Douglas Hildred had been displaying his Spirit lights around the tree and almost managed one by the fairy on the top of the tree. A wonderful evening lasting over two hours, which had thrilled everyone. When we put on the light we found that the children had taken three toys – a plastic car, a celluloid dog and a tin aeroplane, to pass on to some deprived children. As a gesture of friendship, Mr Jones asked that his cigar be sent to Jim McKenzie who had taken our first group of materialisation photographs just a few months earlier and, unbeknown to us at that time of course, would record our Christmas party six years later, on 5th January 1954.

In those days, tape recorders were large, reel-to-reel, bulky and expensive pieces of highly technical audio equipment - way beyond our means, so we were thrilled to accept Jim's kind offer of recording a special circle. The days of cassette recorders were many years away. We naturally invited his wife and youngest son Donald, then in his late 'teens, along with their great friend, Mrs Harrison, no relation to us but a Spiritualist of long standing, whom Jim vouched for. Unfortunately by then Mr Brittain Jones and Dad Hudson had both passed away, in 1953, otherwise we had all our regulars plus Mam Hudson - a very excited party of 11 sitters.

Jim, with the help of his 19-year old son Don, set up his equipment in the corner of our middle room in Oxford Road, with a screen around him to limit the adverse effects of the light from the dials. A microphone cable was laid across the room to my chair so that I could give a running commentary on the one and a half hours' proceedings, the recording of which is the source of this report.

Our tree had been decorated and it stood in the corner to the left of the fireplace. I sat next to my mother with both of us close to the tree. The others sat in the usual semi-circle around the fireplace with Doris occupying my usual position at the other end of the semi-circle to the right of the fireplace. After our prayer and tuneful singing, both Doris and Mrs Harrison having lovely voices, the trumpet phenomena started. Sunrise gave his usual welcome and told us that our Spirit friends were fully aware of what was happening this night. We had of course, received their permission a week or two previously. During this early part of the phenomena we all felt something like confetti falling on us, which turned out to be small apported violets - a lovely welcome.

To accompany our singing, our Spirit friends picked up a small Indian style temple bell, which was standing on the mantelpiece, and vigorously rang it in all areas of the room. I had some difficulty trying to follow the sound with the microphone but managed to record some of the ringing. After a few minutes I heard the bell fall on to the carpet and commented that they had apparently finished with it.

Much to my surprise, about 30 seconds later the ringing started again for a minute or so, and I thought they had picked up the same bell. But not so - and it was

Ivy Hudson, our first trumpet communicator, who told us they had brought us another bell. She said she could tell us who had brought it, but we would find out later.

When we put on the light at the close of the sitting, sure enough, there on the carpet were two bells - both the same style, but the apported one (on the right in the picture at the end of this chapter) was slightly larger than ours - and that is not the only difference. Our original bell, which was probably bought from Woolworth's in the late 1940's, has tarnished quite badly, as you would expect. The apported bell however, even 50 years later, has remained almost as bright as the day it was made! Perhaps the de-materialisation had beneficially affected the molecular structure to retain its colour? It is not really important, but is an interesting observation. The tone is also different and this can be heard on the recording.

As I have said, Ivy Hudson was the first to speak through the trumpet, followed by a William Harrison, an uncle of Mrs Harrison's husband. Margaret McKenzie, Jim McKenzie's grandmother came next and spoke quite well. Mrs McKenzie's mother also came, followed by Sam and his daughter Mona. Sam was particularly pleased because we had not had voices through the trumpet for quite a few months, having all materialisation phenomena, which was not to Sam's liking; and although he did build occasionally, he preferred just to speak.

James Andrew Fleming also paid his annual Christmas visit to repeat his thanks for how we had helped him in 1948. He confirmed that he was now able to enter the family home and believed that his mother knew he was there - happiness and joy for both mother and son.

Sunrise then told us it was "time for the materialisation," so we switched on the red light and Mam was moved back into the corner behind the cabinet curtain. I remained where I was alongside the tree, quite close to the curtain - so close in fact that occasionally I could hear the materialised forms moving behind it before stepping out into the room. We sang for a few minutes before

Sunrise spoke to us from behind the curtain, using an ectoplasmic voice box - not the trumpet. During a previous sitting he had shown us the ectoplasmic voice box he was using. It closely resembled a small rose with the petals moving as he spoke - very interesting.

His first message was to the effect that "the lady can go to the children." We were rather puzzled and I asked him what he meant. He simply repeated the message, so we assumed it was something to do with our family who were in bed. We obtained his permission to open the door of the room to listen for any disturbance and immediately heard Wendy crying - which was not unusual for our 15-month old daughter. Doris asked permission to go and see to her and was told she could return when Wendy had been pacified. Unfortunately it took too long and Doris had to miss the rest of the sitting.

After six years we had got used to having Granny Lumsden as our first materialisation at our weekly sittings, and she did not disappoint us tonight. She pulled the cabinet curtain back with her hand and quickly took the few paces to stand in the centre of the room, immediately in front of the red light, which was hanging from a hook in the ceiling. I leaned forward to hold the microphone as close as I could to her face to record her voice, in exactly the same manner as a radio interviewer. She was her usual cheerful, laughing self, with her surprising opening words of..." 'Ello everybody - how are ya - I told 'em the bairn was crying - yes I told 'em, and you wouldn't have wanted her to cry through all this would ya?" She was obviously referring to Sunrise's comments about Wendy and we thanked her for letting us know. "Well ya know we look after her don't ya?" It is extremely difficult to give a 'true' transcript of a recorded voice with the local accent, and patter, but even if we had not actually seen Granny standing there in the red light, we would certainly have recognised her by her usual 'clipped' Middlesbrough accent in the typical high-pitched voice.

She went on to chat with her daughter, Mam Hudson, telling her that "Charlie's 'ere ya know" - meaning that Dad Hudson had also joined the party. As I have already said in my reports of the weekly sittings, some of us always went over to welcome our Spirit visitors, but had agreed that because of the microphone cable across the floor we would stay in our seats tonight - which Granny commented upon - "It seems funny no one comes over tonight", but added that they all knew why and had been told about the recording! We therefore agreed to let our visitor Mrs Harrison go and meet Granny, who was keen to make sure her face was clearly seen in the red light as she shook hands with Mrs H. - quite a memorable occasion for her.

Granny stayed chatting for a few more minutes and took her leave with her usual "See ya again, ta-ra then, ta-ra," and moved back into the cabinet alongside me. As I am reading this I realise the cold printed word gives no idea whatsoever of the wonderful homely, loving feeling brought by all our Spirit friends and I'm sorry I am unable to do anything to improve such a frustrating situation.

Granny was followed by a rare materialisation of Douglas Hildred, the young man who provided all our Spirit lights - especially tonight with numerous bright twinkling lights actually on the Christmas tree alongside me, outside the cabinet. We understood he had tried to get coloured ones that night but unfortunately could not manage it. I can tell you however that he did manage some coloured lights at later sittings. After a few minutes he found he could not stand the light any longer but continued to speak to us from behind the curtain, giving us this message "I would like to say to the people of your world, Mother, we from the World of Spirit send our greetings to all mankind on your earth. Nearly 2000 years ago a babe was born. If the people of this earth would follow the Christ Principle there would be much more happiness. We from the World of Spirit bring to you, all our love and wish you all Godspeed. Good night, Mother, Good night Gladys, God Bless."

He was followed by Bruce McKenzie, one of Jim's sons, who had passed over as a baby because of a bath-time accident. Now, as a young man in the Spirit World, he wanted to assure his father that it was not his fault. Bruce's grandmother, Margaret Phoenix also built for a moment or two and spoke to her daughter Mrs McKenzie.

Our final materialisation was, as always, Aunt Agg, with her composed, serene presence, speaking to us in her clear, refined yet homely voice. After passing on messages from many Spirit friends present, she assured us that....

"You have given much pleasure to us in the Spirit World. We do like to come and talk to you and pass on our messages from our side of life - and I do hope that those who may be listening to this at any time will be able to be helped and guided by their Spirit friends, as you in this little Circle are helped and guided by yours. From those loved ones of yours who have gone just a step farther - they say they will always be near you, watching you and helping you in this your work for the truth of Spiritualism. Go forth into the world and give your message - a message of Life after Death. Goodnight and God bless you all - Goodnight."

Unfortunately you aren't able to listen to her cultured voice as she had hoped, but I feel the words spoken and faithfully recorded will be of great help to you - as they were to us that night. As you will have gathered, they look forward to be able to come and speak to us - we do *not* "bring them back," as critics of Spiritualism would have it.

After Aunt Agg had returned, Sunrise spoke to us and left a special recorded message for his 'Meedi', as he called my mother, expressing his pleasure to work with her and keeping her in good physical condition to carry on with her work. After Sunrise stopped speaking to us, I lifted the cabinet curtain and my mother soon came out of her deep trance. We then all recorded our parting messages of "Goodnight", including my mother, when suddenly and quite unexpectedly, she went into trance again. Within less than a minute Brownie was speaking to us - quickly and clearly saying "I got the bell for you!" He said he had tried "to get in" earlier but couldn't manage it, so took his chance at the very end - without any discomfort to my mother. A truly wonderful sitting for the benefit of both worlds.

Indian temple bells. The one on the left was in the room all the time and had been damaged by our children playing with it. The larger one on the right was the one brought as an apport during the "Party".

19

Joyful Birthdays

I was recently browsing through Neville Randall's splendid book 'Life after Death', in which he relates some of the stories told by people in the Spirit World through the direct voice mediumship of Leslie Flint. I was interested to read that some of them had lost touch with earthly anniversaries and dates, and were only reminded of them by receiving the thoughts of their loved ones still on the earth. This will no doubt apply to those who have progressed to higher planes, but from the experiences in our Home Circle, those who still have close links with the Earth continue to enjoy sharing such cherished celebrations. This chapter deals with two such instances - the first one concerning my mother while she was still on the Earth, and the other Aunt Agg in the Spirit World.

The most unusual and certainly the largest apport received through my mother's mediumship occurred *not* during a Home Circle sitting, but in my mother's home on her 53rd birthday - 17th March 1948.

This was the time when Mam and Dad had the fish and chip shop and they lived behind the shop. The small kitchen had a walk-in type of pantry with no window, only a zinc-gauze air vent, which was the norm in those days. It was in this semi-dark pantry the exceptional apport occurred. Doris and I, with our five children, lived about 10 minutes drive from the shop. Having already been down in the morning to do the fish preparation and wished Mam a Happy Birthday, I was rather surprised to receive a telephone call from her about four o'clock in the afternoon.

Could I go straight down as there was something unusual she wanted me to see? Nothing more was said and I assumed it was to do with the shop, so I immediately went down. I found Mam and Dad having a cup of tea in the kitchen. Mam usually had a welcoming smile on her face, but on this occasion it seemed a little broader. She realised I would be keen to see why she had telephoned so greeted me with…"Just open the pantry door, son, but be very careful."

Naturally this made me rather curious and not a little apprehensive - but I did exactly as asked. I opened it very slowly but because of the lack of light, for the first few moments could see nothing unusual. Then as I opened it wider to enable me to step inside, I was halted in my tracks!

There at my feet on the floor of the pantry was a mass of lilac blossom - filling the whole area of the floor and as high as the first shelf - about three feet above the ground!

I turned to look at Mam who, with an even bigger grin said, "I thought you'd be surprised" - an understatement if ever there was. But the explanation was even more surprising. Mam had made the customary pot of tea in the afternoon, taken the milk jug out of the pantry, closed the door and sat down on the chair adjacent to the door - which then could not be opened. She quickly realised she had forgotten the sugar, got up and moved the chair and opened the door again - to be confronted by this amazing sight on the pantry floor. A few seconds earlier when she got the milk the floor had been absolutely clear. Now it was packed with lilac blossom. Naturally they were both dumbfounded and Mam's first thought was to ring me. I was as amazed as they were! But where had it come from?

Instinctively I knew it was not a practical joke. Mam and Dad did not do such things and in any case where could they, or anyone else, have collected such a quantity of lilac blossom in mid-March? They had no car and when I removed it, the quantity almost filled the back seat of our medium sized Austin car. I then delivered it in bunches to many of our delighted friends, where it lasted for two or three weeks.

As we had had a few instances of individual flower apports occurring outside the Circle room whilst we were sitting, we did wonder whether the lilac could be a truly exceptional apport while we were not sitting. It really puzzled us all but there seemed no other explanation and we said we would ask our Spirit friends during our sitting three days later on Saturday.

We had naturally told Sydney and Gladys when I delivered the lilac, and they were just as keen as us to ask the question. Aunt Agg materialised, as usual, but before we could say anything, she pre-empted our question by asking us to..."Tell our Min (as she always called my mother) that we have been delighted to be able to bring her such a special birthday gift from her many Spirit friends who are so close to her." Mam of course was just as delighted when we told her at the close of the sitting.

Aunt Agg explained that the darkness of the pantry and the proximity of my mother had afforded ideal conditions for such an unusual apport. It was just another example of her remarkable mediumship - but for a change, this time, she had been the first to witness it! In our excitement we never thought to ask where it had come from, so we still do not know - but lilac certainly does not bloom in the North East of England on 17th March.

The second birthday celebration event was for Aunt Agg herself - on Saturday, the 14th June 1947, which would have been her 62nd anniversary (she passed over in November 1942). On this day her youngest son Terry was married to Ruby Hudson, one of Doris's sisters, at the Middlesbrough Spiritualist Church. Jim McKenzie, known to everyone as Mac, a long-standing friend of both families, conducted the service. The organist was another good friend, Mr Todd, so it was fitting therefore that the McKenzies and the Todds had been invited as guests to our Home Circle sitting that particular evening. The phenomena for both couples proved to be very exciting and evidential.

They had Spirit friends and relatives speaking through the Trumpet, followed by other family members materialising - all of who were recognised and brought messages of great comfort. Finally Aunt Agg materialised, as always, to close the evening's sitting with her cheerful and friendly presence. As she stepped forward from the cabinet, we could all see in the quite bright red light that she was holding five carnations, which she joyfully handed out with her usual well-chosen and suitable words.

One to Mac - "for conducting the ceremony today which meant so much to me."

One to Mrs Mac - "an old dear friend."

One to my wife Doris, to pass on to her sister Ruby, today's bride - "with all my love and best wishes."

One to Mr Todd - "for playing the organ so well."

One to Mrs Todd - to whom she said "I think I knew you as Effie, didn't I, back in St Paul's Road" - which Mrs Todd immediately agreed with. She told us after the sitting, that that was over 15 years before when Aunt Agg had lived in St Paul's Road in Middlesbrough - and even more significant - only Mrs Todd herself knew that, not even her husband.

Aunt Agg then expressed a mother's pleasure about her youngest son marrying such a lovely girl who would look after him and that he had joined such a good, close-knit family. Just before she went I wished her many happy returns of the day and she replied it was the happiest birthday she had ever had! A wonderful evening so appreciated by our guests, so don't forget to send out your thoughts to your loved ones on their special days which can still mean so much to so many of them.

20

Letters from guest sitters

From Dorothy Mattock in Middlesbrough, dated 16ᵗʰ Oct 1947, who was a guest at Sitting 84, 11ᵗʰ Oct. 1947
"May I express my thanks for the wonderful evening I spent with you last Saturday. I have been thinking about everything that happened each day since, and I realize I was very fortunate to have such an experience. My beliefs were confirmed in a very natural and happy way, apart from which, I really enjoyed your pleasant company."

From John Mattock, Dorothy's father who sat with her.
"Please express to the members of your Circle the heartfelt thanks of my daughter and myself for the wonderful manifestations we were honoured to witness on our visit to your Home Circle. Words of mine cannot express the joy and pleasure that I have received at getting positive proof of the future life in such a convincing manner. I sincerely hope the success of your Circle will continue and that you will receive many more visitors and that each will receive such definite proof as we truly received."

From Mrs Lily Dinsdale, a medium in Middlesbrough who held her own Home Circle, letter dated 5.11.53
"I would like to express my very deep appreciation in allowing Mrs Johnson and myself to attend your Circle. It was a great pleasure to shake hands with and speak to my Circle 'chairman', who does some grand work on both

sides of the veil. Mrs Johnson was overjoyed to see her husband and to receive her poetry and flower."

From Mrs Mary Hastie, May 1996

I have already recounted in, 'Living Proof', parts of the next letter from Mrs Mary Hastie of Darlington, who was in the audience the for my talk at Billingham Church, in May 1996, and vividly recalled what her mother, Emily Nicholson, had told her of her experiences as guest sitter in our Circle in 1948 but Mary's letter goes on to say:-

"It was such a pleasure to meet you at Billingham and learn more of the Circle of which my Mum had talked so much. She has been in Spirit for nine years now so I can only give you the facts as I remember them. She told me it was a great privilege to be invited to sit in your mother's Circle and all who were so privileged were very conscious of this.

"Round about the same time, the President of our church, Frank Myers, was invited and was astounded by the materialisations. He had an apport of a pink tulip which he asked Mum to keep for him as he didn't know how to explain it to his wife. Frank passed into spirit in 1963. We have had a photo of the materialised form of your Aunt Agg for a long time, which was given to my mother and she treasured it. Thank you again for a very interesting and enjoyable evening."

My records confirm that Frank Myers was a guest on 14th Feb 1948, Sitting 95, along with Edward Nellist, President of Middlesbrough Church.

Bill Lennie from Middlesbrough, a cousin of Gladys Shipman, was a guest for two successive Sittings, 55 and 56 on the 17th and 24th of May 1947, together with his mother Maud and sister Mildred. He had written to me in December 1989, after reading an article about our Circle in the local 'Evening Gazette', requesting another copy of my first book for a friend. When I sent the book I asked him if he would kindly send me a written statement telling what he could remember of his sittings over 40 years ago. Here are the significant extracts:

"The reason we attended was because at a previous meeting there had been a request from one of the Spirits for my mother to attend....what had previously been a stationary megaphone (the trumpet) suddenly began to whirl about and was the means of audio communication prior to the subsequent materialisation.

I remember vividly two events. Firstly the appearance of Aunt Fanny who was the wife of Uncle Frank, the older brother of Uncle Sam(Sam Hildred). Their son Billie Hildred was serving in the Royal Navy and was rumoured to be involved in various escapades. When I mentioned this to Aunt Fanny she clearly replied "I am watching him." Secondly, was the experiment carried out by Dr. Brittain Jones. Permission was asked and given for a piece to be cut from the ectoplasm for further examination. I can remember the sound as a sharp intake of breath as the doctor made the cut, as any person would if suddenly pricked by a sharp instrument.

To witness the appearance in human form of souls who had departed this worldly life was almost unbelievable, had one not been present. It was a sensational experience, yet the whole atmosphere was one of a cordial family gathering. There was no sense of foreboding, just friendly exchanges. It did demonstrate to me that there is the continuation of another form of life after mortal existence. It did show, how, given the right conditions, that it is possible to establish contact and communicate with the Spirit World and there is nothing to fear from this experience. To me this was truly wonderful."

After one of my talks in Middlesbrough in April 1993, Gwen Schlegel and her sister, Cora Walker, were interviewed and filmed for inclusion in the video made about our Home Circle. I asked them if they would let me have a written record of their memories of the guest sitting in 1954, when they sat, with their mother, Mrs Pearson, and Cora's husband Arnold. Here is what Gwen wrote.

"The materialisation sitting was an experience we shall never forget and feel very privileged that we were given the opportunity to attend. A young man from Spirit came through and demonstrated marvellous lights. Doris's grandmother materialised - a very jolly lady who put everyone at their ease and actually shook hands with each one of us - absolutely wonderful. Mam's sister, Jane, materialised but as this was her first time she found it difficult to stand erect. She said to Cora: 'I love you' which was her usual term of endearment when she was with her, but could only mouth the words when she was in the body. She was very excited finding she was able to speak and called her sister by name - 'Phoebe'. She could not stay long, but this experience was absolutely wonderful. We also had a visit from a mutual friend called Nora who had died whilst she was pregnant. She shook our hands and told us she was very happy and had her baby with her - a little girl. It was wonderful being able to feel her slender youthful hands. Arnold's grandmother also came and gave him some violets.

"These experiences were unforgettable and made a tremendous difference to our lives as we are sure in the knowledge that there is indeed life after this life. I just don't know how people survive the loss of loved ones without the knowledge that we are fortunate enough to share."

(My added comments: The young man providing the lights was, of course, Douglas Hildred, our regular Spirit visitor. As has already been said Jane, had been a deaf mute when on the earth, hence her excitement when she found she could speak when in the materialised body. I too, clearly recall the special way she spoke her sister's name - stressing both syllables..... 'Pheeeee...beeeeee'.)

During one of his occasional calls at my home in late 1988, when I was writing my first book, I had a chat about it with Tony Carr, one of my brothers in law. My notebook showed that he had been a guest at sitting No. 97 on the. 28th February 1948, when he was a rather sceptical eighteen year old. He has spent his professional life in the scientific and technical fields allied to the motor industry. He set up his own successful manufacturing company, and is meticulous in his attention to detail.

He recounted some of his still vivid memories and later wrote me a letter, from which I would now like to quote —

"I found our chat very interesting but also shattering that it was some 40 years ago! Some of the things I had forgotten, but there were two important factors, which I believe are worth recording.

Firstly — before it began Syd advised me to check the whole room to ensure that the only means of access was the door; that the window was closed and blacked out and could not be opened from the outside; and to make sure there were no trap-doors in the floor or ceiling! I can still remember him saying 'People will tell you there were ways of entry into the room. Oh, they will you know!' I must admit I was reluctant to do so but I did it to satisfy Syd, and needless to say, once the door was closed there was no means of entry.

Secondly — the Materialised form of my relative had quite a strong beard and he insisted that I pulled it hard to prove it was not false. I did and there was no way I could detach it from his face! It didn't occur to me at the time that my actions might have caused him some pain — the vigour of my pull would certainly have caused you or I to yell out. But there was no reaction from him.

But to me the most significant part of the evening was the Trumpet movement prior to the commencement of the Spirit voices. The members of the Circle sat around the Trumpet and relatively near to it. In such a small room it was impossible for anyone to move without some of the remaining members being aware of such movement.

I vividly recall the Trumpet slowly rising from the floor (the fluorescent paint on it gave a slight glow in the dark and therefore 'positioned' it for us) and beginning to move around the Circle. It moved up and down in front of each of us, going faster and faster but without ever touching either the floor or our feet. Then it would move up to the ceiling again, never ever touching it. There was no possible way that any sitter could move that physical object so rapidly and diversely, *in the dark.*

As you know Tom, I have spent my working life in the scientific and technical fields and this event remains as the one outstanding experience for which I cannot find, or even imagine, an explanation in physical terms."

Thank you, everyone, for sharing these memories with us.

21

Life goes on

In 1958 my mother sadly lost her battle with cancer, so bringing to an end those wonderful years of the SNC.

That same year, after a few years as a salesman with the Northern Gas Board, I was appointed the area technical representative for a Slough based engineering company – Ronald Trist Ltd. In 1959 they promoted me to National Service Manager which meant a move to Slough area, and we found a house in the lovely village of Eton Wick just across the Thames from Windsor. Such a major move was not an easy decision to make with six children, but it seemed to be advantageous for the family as a whole and so it proved with Colin and Mavis both meeting their future spouses. Unfortunately after four years, personnel moves within the Company made me rather unsettled and after amicable discussions with my Sales Director, we decided to move on again.

This time Doris and I decided to strike out on our own and bought a large property on the sea front in Perranporth, Cornwall where an ex-Army colleague had the local Ironmonger's shop. We spent the winter months of 63/64 completely altering the interior construction to turn it into a 40-seater restaurant. Calling it 'The Cornish Venture', we opened in April 1964. During the following winter period I attended Redruth College to study a catering course and was delighted to obtain a Diploma with Distinction as the top student in the UK.

One of the highlights of our time at the restaurant, which was quite successful, was the day in July 1965 when, as the indirect result of winning a newspaper competition in Middlesbrough thirteen years earlier, Mollie and Jack Warner (Dixon of Dock Green) visited and enjoyed a meal with us. Between serving customers that evening, we had a long discussion about psychic matters. Jack was a close friend of Michael Bentine and both men were extremely interested. Apparently Mollie was a very good medium and Jack told us he accepted no film or TV role without first consulting 'Mollie's little man' – obviously her very close Spirit helper. It was a real pleasure to meet such a genuine and friendly couple and we received Christmas cards from them each year until he passed. Typically, he made one elderly lady's day by signing her menu card and giving her a kiss, as she was leaving the restaurant, when she quietly came over to him and hesitatingly said "It *is* Dixon, isn't it? I watch all your shows " - then turned to her daughter as they went out the door and said triumphantly "I told you it was!"

We would probably have had the restaurant for many years, except my attention was drawn to an advertisement in the Psychic News paper seeking a Manager for the 'Arthur Findlay College for Psychic Science' at Stansted Hall, which was soon to be opened. Arthur Findlay had bequeathed the Hall to the SNU in his will. A College for the study of Psychic Science – what a splendid idea! Something we had needed for many years. After a lengthy interview I was offered the post and at the end of the 'summer season' in Perranporth in October 1966 we sold the business to two friends and moved, with three of our children, to Stansted Hall for me to take up my position as founder Manager of the College. I felt such a key position, in a College helping hundreds of people to develop their Spiritual awareness, would give us tremendous 'job satisfaction' for many years to come.

A very arduous, often frustrating, two years followed, preparing the groundwork for a successful College, We met scores of friendly people including many well known personalities such as Bertha Harris, Ena Twigg, Harry

Edwards and many other excellent speakers and mediums. Unfortunately, as can so often happen amongst volunteer administrators, a most unpleasant 'political intrigue' caused great managerial problems and for the sake of our family's happiness I was ready to leave after the first year. However, at the behest of Bertha's main Guide who controlled her in trance, I was asked to give it another year to see if our Spirit helpers could sort things out.

By the time of her next annual visit however, matters had not improved and her Spirit control thanked me for keeping my side of the bargain but told me I was now free to make my decision. Sadly therefore I resigned and we moved back to Eton Wick in 1968 – terribly disappointed of course but feeling so much happier and more comfortable away from all the unpleasantness at the College at that time. I later heard that the situation continued for a long time afterwards.

One significant outcome of our stay at Stansted was the fact that, at the behest – no, 'command' is a better word – of Fanny Higginson, Gordon's very mediumistic mother, I started my illustrated talks about the Saturday Night Club physical phenomena, which led to scores of visits to churches and centres throughout the UK. It was during November 1966, before the College was officially open, while we were enjoying an evening's relaxation in the lounge with a few guests. Amongst them was Gordon Higginson, the exceptional medium who, some years later became Principal of the College, and his mother Fanny, also an outstanding medium who had 'developed' Gordon's gift as a boy medium at Longton Church in the Potteries. Gordon and I were of an age, about 48, and Fanny would have been in her late sixties.

We were chatting about things in general with particular reference to the future of the College which was due to receive its first students before the end of the year, when Fanny, who was sitting next to me suddenly turned and said "There's a strong smell of fish and chips here. Does that mean anything to you Tom?" " Yes," I said, "I can understand that". Then she went on, pointing her hand in the air above where Doris was sitting, "There is a beautiful archway there with the letters M. I. N. round the top."

"Yes," I said again, "my mother's name was Minnie, often called Min, and she had a fish and chip shop before she passed to the higher life about eight years ago."

This I thought was very good evidence that my mother was with us in the College and I started telling Fanny about our wonderful Home Circle in Middlesbrough. I told her about my mother's remarkable physical mediumship which allowed us to experience so many forms of physical phenomena, the apports, spirit lights, spirit writing, telekinesis, spirit voices through the Trumpet, culminating in full sized ectoplasmic spirit materialisations.

Her enthusiasm, when she saw the photographs we had taken in the Circle, knew no bounds. The diminutive Fanny, in her most matriarchal manner, which Gordon knew only too well, told me to get myself to a photographer and have some slides made from the photographs. "Then," she said, "get round the country giving talks about your wonderful experiences. You can't keep this to yourself, it must be spread as far as possible for everyone to know." And when Fanny, all 5 feet 2 inches of her, commanded, you just had to obey!

The following morning I had to go into Bishop's Stortford on business, so I took the opportunity to call at the local photographic shop run by a young Mr Harris. I asked him whether he could make slides from photographic prints, which were almost 20 years old. He answered that he could but would obviously like to examine them. So with some trepidation I handed over the black and white prints of ectoplasmic phenomena (as included in this book), wondering what his reaction would be. Imagine my complete surprise when he simply said, "Oh, ectoplasmic materialisations. Are you from Spook Hall?"

"Yes" I replied, feeling greatly relieved by his response, "I am the Manager of the Arthur Findlay College at Stansted Hall" (the Hall had soon become locally known as Spook Hall - for obvious reasons,) "but how do you know about such matters?" I asked him. "Oh, my grandmother was a medium and I've always been interested in such things." Rather an unexpected reply, but an immediate friendly relationship was established, and he made me two sets of excellent slides, which are still in use today, almost 40 years later. They have seen me through over 150 talks across the British Isles, Portugal and Spain, with audiences ranging from 10 to 120. Fanny arranged one of my first talks in Leicester, and thanks to her 'command', thousands of interested people have shared with me those remarkable experiences of physical phenomena through my mother's very special mediumship.

We moved back to Eton Wick. My old Company in Slough, heard I was in the area and offered me the post of Export Office Manager. I enjoyed this for about 18 months before I was asked to become Accounts Office Manager, a post which I also enjoyed in those pre-computerisation days. My training and membership of the British Institute of Management was proving most useful, especially when there were 'trouble-shooting' problems.

As soon as they decided to computerise the accounts they brought in an 'expert' and I left to operate as a 'free lance' accountant. This enjoyable pathway I continued until my 'gradual retirement' around 1988. The free-lance work for small companies also enabled me to spend more 'quality' time with Doris. We travelled widely in Europe thanks to most of the family working at British Airways. Doris was struck by cancer and passed over in 1976 aged 59 − a sad physical loss to all the family after 36 happily married years.

At that time I was still enjoying travelling the country giving my illustrated talks. I had been frequently asked at the end of my talks whether I had written a book, which they could take away with them. I kept promising myself, and my audiences, that I would do something about it, but unfortunately, owing to the usual rounds of everyday activities, some 20 years elapsed before I finally acted. As my New Year's resolution, on January 1st 1988, I started the first page. I would reach my 'three score years and ten' that August, and my 'shelf life' was coming up fast or as another friend put it 'you are now in *extra time*'. It took over a year to complete the book, which covered, very briefly, a few of the remarkable happenings in our Home Circle, and included four of the photographs. My youngest daughter Wendy, a computer tutor, came up to my office one lunch time to find me typing and 'tippexing' away on my old typewriter. She promptly told me I should use her word processor at her home. I shuddered a little at the very thought but was persuaded to go and have an introductory lesson which resulted in my going to her place every day for many months to write over 20 short chapters about our experiences in the Saturday Night Club.

The finished book 'Visits by Our Friends from the Other Side' was printed, for me, by a friend in April 1989 on the very week I was invited, as the Founder Manager of the Arthur Findlay College, to give three talks during their celebrations for the 25th Anniversary of the College. I was delighted to sell 100 copies during that first week, which gave my Cancer Fund a splendid start.

About five years after the publication of the book, and many talks later, my middle daughter, Joyce, said to me "You can't go on giving your talks round the country Dad." I quickly asked "Why not?" "Well you're getting on a bit now, (I was an active seventy five!) so you had better get a video made!" A video! What a crazy idea! How would you approach it? Who do you contact? How much would it cost? Yes, a splendid idea Joyce, but 'not on'- we thought.

In June 1993 I was asked by the sociologist and writer Joe Cooper to give my talk at a Day School he was holding in Wakefield. I stayed overnight with a very friendly couple, Antony and Patricia Hamblin, on the edge of Wakefield. Tony, with a Ph.D. in Organic Chemistry, had retired from his senior post at Leeds Polytechnic, now Leeds Metropolitan University, whilst Pat had been Organiser for Adult Education in the Wakefield area. We got on very well together and they came with me to my talk on physical phenomena, about which they knew nothing. On the morning after the talk we were having coffee in their garden when Pat mentioned that part of her work involved making training videos for the Wakefield College - and as they say, the rest is history. The crazy idea was now not quite so crazy. With Pat's expertise on the production and editing side, and Tony's excellent camera work, the bulk of the work was done within 12 months. They filmed and recorded five of my talks at different venues throughout the UK and did personal interviews with Sydney and Gladys Shipman at Robin Hood's Bay.

After my talk in Middlesbrough they interviewed sisters Gwen Schlegel and Cora Walker, both of whom had been guests in our Home Circle some 40 years previously and assured us it had 'changed their lives'. Further interviews with me as the 'link man' meant quite a hectic number of months for Pat and Tony but they never complained - in fact they said they really enjoyed it all, and I cannot thank them enough for all the splendid work they did.

After some excellent professional 'post production' work with Howard Garton in Kirkella, near Hull, the final 60-minute video was out on sale in October 1995 and Joyce's 'impossible dream' had come true. Howard also helped us to have 200 audiotapes professionally produced, of our 'Christmas Party' sitting in January 1954. Extracts of this tape have been now been made into a half hour programme by Chris Eldon Lee, a Radio programme producer, for a BBC Radio 4 broadcast for Christmas Eve in 2003, entitled 'Christmas Spirits'.

Since I started, thanks to my talks in the main, I have sold over 5,000 books, almost 1,000 videos and raised much money for Cancer victims. All proceeds from the sales have always gone into my personal Cancer relief fund, through which I have been so pleased to be able to help directly so many sufferers at what I call 'grass roots' level, where say £100 direct to the individuals, or the small Support Groups, has in some small way improved the quality and dignity of their shattered lives. Apart from my cancer fund greatly benefiting, the Truth has been spread to hundreds more people who have been unable to attend my talks, thanks to the great support we have received from our Spirit friends who keep us going.

After the trip to Wakefield I visited a new Spiritual Centre near Howden in East Yorkshire which resulted in meeting Ann, who has been a tremendous loving support, when we were still touring the UK giving my talks and especially now in my 'senior years'. We married in 1998 and welcomed in the new Millenium by moving to Spain in January 2000. Apart from enjoying the sunshine, we have continued our Spiritual development with many friends, still giving the occasional talk and have spent a lot of time planning and writing this book, which I trust you will enjoy.

I feel I am a privileged man having had such wonderful experiences, and am very keen to let the world know the Truth of Life after Death. As Sir William Crookes, the renowned scientist said after his years of test séances –
"We don't say these things are possible – only that they occur".

And so they did for us – time and time and time again – and I was so privileged to be part of it.

In the grounds of Stansted Hall 1996

Signing books after a talk on my mother's mediumship, 1998

Four generations of my family at my 85th Birthday Party, 2003

The Stewart Alexander Circle celebrates Katie's book launch

22

Susan's Greetings

Our eldest son Colin, born in 1942, married his first wife Margaret in October 1965 at a lovely old parish church in the village of Eton Wick, close by Eton College near Windsor. After a number of years hoping for a child they were blessed with the birth of Susan in February 1971. They were of course thrilled, and a very happy and devoted family - until December 1973 when tragedy struck. Margaret, then a young woman of 38 had to go into Windsor hospital for a minor internal operation. She was due for discharge a few days before Christmas, but 12 hours before Colin was to collect her, she had a severe relapse and died in the early hours of December 22nd. A traumatic shock to us all - but especially to Colin, who was now left with a daughter, not yet three years old.

Doris and I persuaded Colin to come and stay with us for a few months, so that Nanna Doris, who was not only a registered nurse and midwife, but had already brought up a family of six, could help to care for Susan while he was coming to terms with such a sudden and devastating loss. Fortunately he has always had a mature and philosophical outlook on life and is the kind of man who can handle such crises. Having been brought up in a Spiritualist family he knew that Margaret was still living in the Spirit World and when she was ready would still be helping to care for their daughter - who was truly the 'apple of her eye'.

Although the family (Colin being the eldest of six) and many friends were unstinting with their support, Colin was keenly aware that the loss of her mother would prove very difficult for Susan, then almost three years old - particularly as she started mixing with other children who were accompanied by their mothers. But fortune smiled again when after a year or so he was introduced to another Margaret who, a few years previously had lost her husband with a heart attack, leaving her with two young daughters aged about five and seven years. The friendship quickly blossomed and we were delighted when they married in March 1975 and became a truly splendid family. Susan now had a Mum and Julie and Lorraine had a Dad. Happy days once more.

In November 1980, Colin, an engineer with British Airways at nearby Heathrow, had the opportunity to emigrate to South Africa where Margaret had a married sister Barbara with family in Durban. Colin's new employers, an aircraft engineering company near Johannesburg, arranged temporary accommodation for them and the first 12 months were filled with the excitement of finding and moving into their own home on the outskirts of Boksburg, near Johannesburg, with all the accompanying changes relating to a different culture - especially the schools for the three girls. From their letters and telephone calls it was a hectic but very happy and satisfying time.

Until on Friday December 4th 1981, only 12 months after their arrival. Susan now 10 years old, was admitted in the morning to a local clinic for the removal of her tonsils; a simple routine operation, in and out the same day. Very sadly something went wrong in the theatre. Tragedy had struck again!

I received a call from Colin, about 8 am. UK time, telling me that Susan had passed away under the anaesthetic an hour or so previously. Another tremendous shock! Not only had he lost the physical presence of his first wife unexpectedly some eight years previously, but now he had lost their only child. True to his character however, he simply commented that at least he still happily had his second wife Margaret and her two girls, while his first wife Margaret now had their daughter in the Spirit World.

A truly Spiritual outlook under such devastating circumstances, but one which would be of great help to others suffering in the same way. I can also add that in addition to her mother, Susan would be met by Colin's mother, my late wife affectionately known as Nanna Doris, who passed over in April 1976.

It was some weeks before I could fly out to see them but we kept in close telephone contact, and I now append a brief resumé, as recorded by Colin each day, of some remarkable happenings which occurred in their bungalow in Beyer's Park over a period of 16 days - starting two days after Susan's passing. Colin, Margaret and the two girls, then in their mid-teens, are very much down-to-earth - not subject to fantasising or making up stories. Both the girls have since held senior management positions in banking and the computer world - so I am quite certain that what Colin told me actually did happen.....strange as it may seem!

He used to ring me every day to report and after the second call I impressed on him to write down immediately the facts as they happened, as memory can play tricks. This account is based on those written notes.

Sunday 6ᵗʰ Dec.1981 - two days after Susan's passing. During the evening, as they were relaxing in the lounge, Colin and Margaret noticed a half-eaten peach behind a large glazed pot on the hearth of the fireplace in the lounge area. This obviously puzzled them and they were suspicious that it may have been caused by a mouse as they had found a nest in the kitchen that morning. But nowhere, neither then nor afterwards, were there any signs of a mouse or mouse-droppings in the bungalow.

Furthermore, the fruit was always kept in a large bowl on a table in the dining area - about 12 feet from the hearth - a long distance for a mouse to move a peach. I should explain that the living room is an open area about 35 feet long, with the dining area of about 10 feet at one end. The door to the corridor and bedrooms is at the junction between the dining area and the lounge and is opposite the fireplace, about 15 feet away.

Monday 7ᵗʰ Dec. - Margaret's sister Barbara, like Margaret a woman in her forties, had arrived from Durban and stayed until Monday the 21ˢᵗ, when they all went to Barbara's home for a two to three week holiday. So Barbara was also a witness to these unusual happenings.

The 'happenings' occurred during the night when everyone was asleep and the results were seen when they entered the living room the following morning. On this particular morning they found one half-eaten peach and one whole peach on the hearth. Neither showed signs of bruising, which would have occurred if they had been dropped or fallen. Again they were very puzzled, but did recall that whilst Susan liked all kinds of fruit, peaches were her favourite. Naturally the girls were questioned but assured their parents that they knew nothing about the fruit being moved.

Tuesday 8ᵗʰ Dec. - Nothing to report.

Wednesday 9ᵗʰ Dec. - Another half-eaten peach on the hearth - and I must emphasise that after they had a close examination of the area, the 'evidence' was removed each morning.

By now they were becoming very intrigued and checked amongst themselves that no one had been up during the night, and no one was subject to sleepwalking. There were two guard dogs kept in a separate part of the garden and they were never allowed in the house. Because they were all so intrigued and puzzled, they specially left three peaches in the bowl on the dining table before going to bed and they agreed that they would all wait for each other and enter the room together the following morning.

Thursday 10th Dec. - On entering the room together they found two of the peaches half-eaten on the hearth and there was no sign of the third one at that time. It was only later that day that Margaret found it on the floor behind one of the easy chairs in the lounge area about 14 feet from the table.

Friday 11th Dec. - Margaret had bought some cherries and put them in the fruit bowl on the dining table. She also bought a small Christmas tree, removed the glazed pot from the hearth in the lounge area and put the tree in its place. Nothing happened today or on the following day - Saturday 12th.

Sunday 13th Dec. - This morning they found two whole cherries and one cherry stone on the hearth near the tree.

Monday 14th Dec. - The tree had been decorated on the Sunday and this morning they found two baubles, undamaged, on the hearth. They were quite sure that the baubles could not have just fallen off the tree as they had been fixed quite securely, and if they had fallen they would most likely have broken.

Tuesday 15th Dec. - Nothing to report.

Wednesday 16th Dec. - Nothing to report, but before going to bed that night they especially left half a fresh fig from their own garden on the dining table.

Thursday 17th Dec. - This morning the fig had gone and there were just a few scraps on the table where it had been placed. More amazement - so before going to bed that night they filled the bowl with nine plums, four oranges and one apple - a change from the peaches, cherries and figs.

Friday 18th Dec. - On entering the room they were astounded to see that the four oranges and the apple were still there - but the nine plums had completely vanished, and after a very thorough search they found neither plums nor stones - not then or since !

So before going to bed, Colin suggested they left another of their own figs and this time he said specifically "For Susan" - whereupon Margaret cut it in half and put it on a plate on the dining table.

Saturday 19th Dec. - This time, one half of the fig had gone and the other half was on the floor by the table. By now their excitement was difficult to contain, especially the two girls, so in the evening Julie peeled an orange, separated it into eight segments and put them on a plate on the dining table. Again they said "For Susan." As they were still concerned about the 'mouse aspect' in all these happenings, they laid some mouse bait and one of the girls was heard to say - "Be careful Susan, don't eat those or they will kill you!" At which, of course, they all had a good laugh!

Sunday 20th Dec. - This morning they found five segments still on the plate, one on the tabletop, one on the hearth and one completely vanished - never found.

Unfortunately they were unable to continue with their observations as they had previously arranged to go to Durban with Barbara on 21st Dec. and were understandably a little disappointed after so much excitement. Nothing similar occurred in Durban - but as they entered their driveway on their return, they were quite startled and apprehensive to see that the wrought iron security gate fitted on the *inside* of their locked glass front door (a standard fitment in South Africa) was standing ajar!! They were quite certain that they had securely locked it before leaving for Durban, which was something they always double-checked.

They immediately thought that there had been a break-in and approached the house very cautiously. But to their amazement and great relief they found nothing whatsoever amiss. After much questioning and serious discussion amongst themselves, they finally came to the happy conclusion that it was Susan's way of saying "Welcome Home." The thought that it could have been intruders frightened Margaret so much that she asked Susan not to do it again and that was the last of the unusual happenings in Beyer's Park.

The sceptics will offer all kinds of reasons for such happenings, which are usually far more difficult to accept than the simple Truth which Colin and his family are quite sure about - that Susan and her mother Margaret were letting them know that they were very much alive and sharing Christmas with them.

Perhaps I may add, that as Grandparents, my wife, Doris, and I had felt that throughout her short life here Susan always appeared to be 'an old head on young shoulders' and when sitting quietly by herself often seemed to be in another world - perhaps the world she now enjoys.

Now, 20 years later, I had another amazing 'happening' linked with Susan. At that time Ann and I were members of a small spiritual group here in Spain where one of the group members was a trance medium. During the meeting, in early December 2001, just before we were leaving for a visit to Colin and Margaret in South Africa, a young girl communicator spoke to us through our medium and asked us to sing a Christmas carol - with which we duly obliged.

We were sitting in a darkened room so could see almost nothing of the surroundings, but during the singing I felt something drop on to my left foot (I always remove my shoes when sitting in such a group). I commented on this to the spirit communicator and she simply said that when we sing carols we get money for presents - so she had brought me some money! All I can say is that it did not feel like a coin when it hit my foot but it was probably in a 'psychic pocket' to protect it.

The communicator added that in fact it had been brought by the 'little girl' attached to me who had now grown up in the Spirit World - Susan! Wonderful! When we put on the light at the end of the meeting there was a small silver coloured coin on the floor between my feet. When we examined it we found it was a 10 Sen coin from Malaysia dated 1981.

Not only was this a wonderful apport for us but think on these facts.....

The date of our meeting was 4th December - the date Susan passed.

The year on the coin was 1981 - the year Susan passed.

The coin value was 10 sen. - and Susan was 10 years old when she passed - date of birth being 26.2.71.

We have no idea where this coin came from but it is now a treasured possession amongst our other interesting apports and memorabilia, a special memory of Susan.

~~~~

Lamps of happiness

Make this New Year sweeter to remember
By all the kind things you think and do;
For there are hearts much colder than December
Who truly need someone just like you.
Hearts which once were lit with Hope's bright candles
Which shone with laughter like a golden song –
YOU can give them something to remember
Because your Love just came along.
So send your thoughts to shine across Life's darkness
And they will reach much farther than you guess,
To make this New Year sweeter to remember
And light again the Lamps of Happiness.

<div align="right">M.R.H.</div>

23

Other 'Close Encounters'

'Physical phenomena' can occur anywhere, anytime, when the conditions are suitable. It is likely to be occurring in your own homes or surroundings without your realizing it at the time. How often have you found things moved from where you knew you had put them, into perhaps another room in the house - like car keys, pens, hair brushes, spectacles etc.? It could just be friendly Spirit children having fun with you or loved ones letting you know they are close, but be assured, in a normal friendly home, they will not knowingly cause you harm or concern. Of course, there are mischievous Spirits around, but their 'misdeeds' are few and far between and the following story shows how we are looked after by our loved ones around us.

In 1950 Doris and I were living in a terraced house in Oxford Road, Middlesbrough with our family of five children with ages ranging from three to nine years, and had little money to spare. Doris in fact had become very adept at making a little go a very long way.

She always folded the few pound notes individually in her purse and always knew how many she had. When at home she left her purse on a high shelf on the Welsh dresser in the living room. I came home one evening to find her very upset because she was fairly certain that a pound note was missing from her purse.

She had questioned all the children and they had assured her that they were not involved. Doubts of all kinds pass through parents' minds at times like this, but we had no reason not to believe them – and left it at that.

Naturally we were still concerned that we had lost about one sixth of our weekly income – and still rather puzzled. Doris checked and rechecked her spending and was still fairly certain that a pound was missing – but we said nothing to anyone else.

Come the following Sunday evening however we had a most unexpected and pleasant surprise – although by now, after four years of the remarkable phenomena in our Home Circle, we should not have been so surprised. But this occasion was slightly different and was not during one of our sittings.

Mam and Dad used to visit us for tea most Sundays and stay to watch the regular weekly play on television. There was always an 'Interlude' during the play (the ploughing horses, the playful kitten, etc.) when Doris would make the usual cup of tea. On this particular Sunday, Doris popped into the kitchen and I was sitting next to Mam, ready to have a little chat. Within 30 seconds, before I could say anything, however, she was in trance, eyes closed, and Aunt Agg was speaking to us. The sisters had such a close psychic rapport that it was as simple as that.

She told me that she was fully aware of our concern about the missing pound note and firstly assured us that none of our children was involved. I called Doris back from the kitchen and Aunt Agg then proceeded to tell us what had actually happened.   Because of the strength of the psychic power in our house, Spirit people could easily use it to move things around, as we had often noticed. Harmless fun by the Spirit children, which we never discouraged and usually had a good laugh about. But on this occasion things were different.

This time it was a young boy, recently passed over, who had not been averse to 'nicking' the odd item when on the earth and his outlook had not had time to change since his passing. This is quite normal and poltergeists are an extreme example of this inability to understand their change of state - from earthly to Spirit beings.

He had taken the note from Doris's purse with the intention of keeping it but because of the protective 'psychic aura' provided by our close Spirit helpers, he found he could not take it out of the house and had therefore just left it. Aunt Agg then told us he had actually left it under the refrigerator in the kitchen - probably thinking he was hiding it and would not be 'found out'.

I thanked Aunt Agg very much indeed and said I would immediately retrieve it. She said she would wait until we had actually recovered it and had been only too pleased to be able to help - especially to clear the bairns, as she called them.

Sure enough, by raking under the one-inch gap below the fridge with a long garden cane, *the pound note came out!!* together with much dust and fluff of course! And it was still folded in Doris's usual way. Aunt Agg then chuckled in her inimitable way, said 'Cheerio' and within another 30 seconds mother came out of her trance, We still had time for our cup of tea before the end of the 15 minute interval, and we were then able to tell Mam all about it. Remember, she knew nothing about the affair until we told her after Aunt Agg had gone and she was just as pleased as we were to hear of the 'happy ending'. Just another example of their closeness, always amongst us and show their caring when it is needed. They are still part of our family and act in the same way that families do - by helping whenever possible. But they do not interfere and run our lives for us - that is always our own personal responsibility.

On another occasion the Sunday play was set in France and as we watched my mother kept saying I know this place. 'You can't', we told her, 'you've never been out of England!' But she insisted that she did know it and kept telling us what was round the corner.

When the 'Interlude' came on and the Potter's Wheel started turning Doris went through to the kitchen to put the kettle on and we sat chatting. Within a few seconds my mother's eyes closed and a familiar smile appeared on her lips. "Hello, Aunt Agg," I said.

"I've just popped in to let you know why 'Our Min' thinks she knows the place in the play", she said.

"Are you watching the television?" I asked incredulously.

"Oh yes" she said, "we do when it is interesting and one of Min's guides who works with her is a doctor named Jean Dupré, who lived in that village. He is here now, impressing her about his old home town". A simple explanation and shows how 'nudges' from the Spirit World might construed as our own thoughts!

The story of the pound note is rather exceptional, but I have experienced many other 'happenings' of a similar nature - one of which occurred in South Africa on New Year's Day 1998. Ann and I were visiting my eldest son Colin and his wife Margaret. We were all having a few days holiday together at a ranch-style hotel near Sun City, some two hours drive away from their home. We planned to have breakfast at the Game Park Lodge, before doing a 'game drive' and as this meant a 6 am. start the cases were packed and closed the day before.

After a very hot day, spent viewing zebra and antelope etc. we arrived at the Hotel with thoughts of diving straight into the hotel pool. Imagine my surprise when I lifted the neatly folded shirts and shorts off the top of the case to see a shining 50-cent coin (dated 1996) lying on the grey shoe bag beneath. I left the case as it was and called to Ann that I had taken the shirts out of the case, and asked her to bring her camera. She came to find her swimwear and, seeing the coin, said, "Why have you put that there?" "I haven't. It was there when I lifted the shirts out," I replied. A photograph was taken immediately for record purposes and the coin is in our memorabilia.

No money was put in the suitcase when we packed. The shirts and shorts were all clean so there was no money in the pockets, and Ann certainly hadn't seen it when she neatly packed everything the day before.

Where it came from we never found out but accepted it as simply another sign that our loved ones were with us. I suppose I was not too surprised, especially with Susan's frequent close presence, as you will gather from the previous chapter, and we all had a most enjoyable holiday.

May you too be aware of and enjoy the same closeness of your loved ones, particularly when you may be celebrating or perhaps more importantly, when feeling the need of comfort.

24

Stewart Alexander

It was in 1989 that I received a letter from a gentleman called Stewart Alexander who lived near Hull. He had learned about my Christmas Party audiotape, which had been recorded 1954 and wondered whether he could have a copy to include in his extensive library of psychic phenomena, which he had collected over many years of investigation. I explained to Stewart that (a) I had only one copy of the 'old fashioned' type of reel-to-reel tapes which had not been transferred to the current cassette type and (b) I could not give such permission without agreement from the two surviving members of the SNC - Sydney and Gladys Shipman who lived in Robin Hood's Bay, near Whitby.

Stewart was so keen that within a few weeks he and his close friend Ray Lister arranged to visit the Shipmans to obtain their approval, which was given without hesitation. Sydney and Gladys were most impressed with the credibility of Stewart and Ray who had been sitting in a physical phenomena Circle for a number of years with gradually improving results. So now it was up to me to try to find some means of transferring the reel-to-reel tapes to cassettes. Stewart kindly offered to pay the cost of such work but we agreed to share it as it would be of value to both of us.

After many months of enquiries I eventually found a 'one-man' company in Bracknell who had the suitable equipment for this kind of transfer, which resulted in a two-cassette copy that I still have.

I promptly made a second copy and posted it to Stewart for which he was extremely grateful and we became good friends, exchanging regular correspondence. We first met in January 1991 at the inaugural meeting of the Noah's Ark Society where I gave my illustrated talk about materialisation, which was repeated at the Leicester meeting and again at Wimbledon some months later.

My mother had been in the Spirit world for over 30 years, and I had certainly felt the loss of our regular weekly sittings - so you can imagine my delight when I received Stewart's invitation to sit as a privileged guest in his Home Circle in Hull. They told me that they had trumpet phenomena and deep trance control communication through Stewart, but had not developed any ectoplasmic materialisations such as we had been privileged to experience in our own Home Circle.

At that time I was living near High Wycombe in Bucks, so had about a 400 miles return journey, with an overnight stay kindly arranged by Ray Lister. I was more than willing and happy to undertake such a journey for an opportunity to renew my contact with our Spirit friends in a physical Circle. With my experiences throughout the years of the Saturday Night Club, I was certainly not seeking personal proof, which I had already received in abundance. In addition to my personal pleasure and thrill of being involved again in a physical Circle, I hoped I might be able to have a constructive and contributory input for the benefit of the Circle as a whole. Sunrise had always told me I was a strong source of psychic power and energy.

Stewart was delighted when I requested permission to take along our trumpet. So on the 19th April 1993 I joined the eight other regular sitters in a specially prepared room in Ray and June Lister's home in Hull. I was inwardly excited of course, especially as we had our trumpet alongside theirs - both clearly distinguished by means of their luminous spots, which had been painted on the bell ends. The hour and a half sitting took place in complete darkness, exactly the same as I was accustomed to in the early days of our Saturday Night Club sittings with trumpet phenomena only. I have a seven page transcript of the tape recording made during that sitting, which for me, was a unique occasion to witness again trumpet phenomena in a Home Circle other than our own almost 47 years previously. I was made extremely welcome by both the sitters and the Spirit visitors who spoke to us, including the 'Circle Controller', Stewart's Spirit guide White Feather; 'young' Christopher, whose purpose was, and still is, to make everyone laugh to lift the vibrations, with the stalwart, assertive, yet always very friendly Walter Stinson, all of whom, along with Freda Johnson who joined the Circle later, have since become very close Spirit friends.

It would be impracticable to report all the evening's events but there are a few worthy of recall. White Feather opened the sitting with a very warm welcome; followed by Christopher chatting in his own inimitable way, and Walter briefly introducing himself, saying he would return later. He was followed by the extremely quiet voice of a lady belonging to that renowned and famous medium, Mrs Osborne Leonard, who apologised for taking some time to have full control because there was so much being done while she was speaking. It was indeed an exciting moment to meet such a well-known lady who then addressed me personally:

"Mr Harrison, we have something of a surprise which we would like to bring to you later if we may. We know that you have been looking forward to this evening and we ourselves have been looking forward to your visit. There are one or two people who are particularly anxious to speak with you." She continued to comment on my background and the value of my talks around the country, and hoped that in some small way tonight they could reward me. I was certainly not seeking any reward but eagerly anticipating the unfoldment of the evening's events. Mrs Leonard then gave words of encouragement to Denise Lister, to whom she had become closely attached and hoped to work through her.

Christopher returned and said: "There's a bloke running up and down here with a bucket of water. Tom, this means something to you." I was trying to think of someone who may have been connected to the fire services when Christopher added: "He says there's something in the Circle belonging to him." I promptly replied, "The trumpet?", which by now was suspended in mid-air. "Who's Running Water - he hasn't been for a long time," said Christopher. "True," I said, "he is Aunt Agg's main Spirit guide who used to use this trumpet in her Home Circle in the 1930's."

Splendid evidence so soon in the sitting.

At this point our trumpet was whirling round the room, clearly seen by the four luminous spots on the bell end. Sunrise, my mother's main Spirit guide then gave his sign of a circle, clockwise and anti-clockwise as he always did, before the trumpet stopped immediately in front of me. It then waved up and down, gently pushed me in the stomach, rolled across both my hands and finally on my head. You will no doubt appreciate that by now I was very excited and could only keep repeating "Excellent, brilliant, wonderful..." etc.' Then both trumpets moved in unison very rapidly around the room - and much further from the medium than ever before - according to all the sitters' excited comments. Christopher added: "It's because Tom has brought some power." "Thank you Christopher."

Stewart's trumpet was now suspended at head height on the other side of the room, while ours was just above knee high pointing towards me and Gaynor, Stewart's sister sitting on my right, who was adjacent to Stewart. Gaynor and I could just hear from our trumpet, a quiet voice that proved to be my mother saying "My boy" and what sounded like 'Sonny'. This was what she called me until I was about 10 years old, and even in later years often called me 'Sonner', which was unknown to anyone else in that room. She finished with a very loud kissing noise - typical of my mother. What we had not realised at the time was that the same message was being relayed through the other trumpet to the sitters on the other side of the room - stereophonic sound for the first time in Stewart's circle - something a bit special enjoyed by all the sitters! As Christopher excitedly explained: "The voice box was connected to both of them - that's not happened before - exciting stuff - I told you we were trying something different."

Sunrise then gave his welcome sound through the trumpet and by now I had been transported back to the wonderful sittings with the Saturday Night Club almost 50 years ago! The next voice, also rather quiet, completely surprised me - "Doing my best - can't think - have spoken before, not here - Tom, young Tom, do you no recognise me - can you no hear me (Yes) Willie (Willie Earle?) Yes - a long time ago - I've no changed, just got older - I've waited 40 years for this!"

Another special voice from the past, which I have told you about, in Sitting 73.

By the time Uncle Jack had spoken and tapped me on my head with the trumpet, I was truly exhilarated and thoroughly enjoying such a remarkable evening. The voices continued to come through both trumpets and after three more Spirit people had spoken we saw in a dim red light, an ectoplasmic hand holding a plaque, with Christopher saying "We wanted to make it memorable for Tom". As I replied, it could not have been more memorable. He then added "Send our love to Sydney and Gladys; they're nice aren't they." "Yes, I'll be seeing them tomorrow" I replied.

The trumpets then returned to the floor and we had a long discourse from a gentleman called Jack who controlled Stewart fairly often. He was very close to Christopher and used to take him fishing. He spoke very clearly and after welcoming me stated that they were all delighted with tonight's results. My extra power had made such a difference. Christopher then came back controlling Stewart to add: "The power's gone very low - we've done our best - Tom, you can come again (I'd like to) - well I've invited you (Thank you) - I think it's been lovely - people over here have been ever so pleased - they said you've waited a long time (Yes) - Your Mum's lovely, she did a lot of work when she was on your side - that's why we've tried to give her a reward - can't hang on now - bye, bye."

White Feather returned to give his blessing…."You will all go from here knowing that you have love over in our world. Goodnight." One of the other sitters closed in prayer and the sitting ended at 9.40 pm.

The joyful comments from all the sitters afterwards simply echoed my own innermost feelings of a wonderful conjoining of both worlds - the purpose of the Saturday Night Club, which I had truly missed since my mother's passing in November 1958. I proffered my sincere thanks to Stewart and all the sitters, hoping that I would be able to make another visit to such a sincere and harmonious Home Circle - which came to pass some eight weeks later on 15th June - another wonderful evening.

At that time, because of the preponderance of my talks in the north of England and Scotland, my schedule meant I was in the Hull area about every four or five weeks, and Ann and I were fortunate enough to be invited to sit with Stewart in January 1994 - Ann's first sitting in a physical circle. The invitation became an open one for us whenever I was in the area and we sat at least once per month during '94 and for the first six months of '95. Shortly after August 1995, when I had moved to live with Ann at Swanland, close to the Humber Bridge, we became regular members of this unique Home Circle in Hull. We thoroughly enjoyed the weekly sittings until our move to Spain in January 2000 when we were endowed with 'permanent honorary membership' to join our friends whenever we were in the Hull area during our visits to the UK - keenly anticipated evenings - the jewels in the crown! Our sincere thanks and gratitude go to Stewart and Ray for making these things possible, together with our very dear friends in both worlds.

Stewart's Home Circle, with a few changes in the members, has been sitting for some 30 years and the physical phenomena is progressively developing, as will be confirmed by all those privileged people who have sat with him so often in his public demonstrations throughout the past decade. I understand that when the Circle first started they were concentrating on Stewart's brother Michael as the potential medium, but it gradually became clear that the Spirit people wanted to work through Stewart, whose mediumship now includes:

- noisy telekinesis with drum sticks and small bells;

- whirling trumpet movements and Spirit voices through the trumpet;

- a variety of experiments carried out by the ever-active and forward-looking Walter Stinson, one of Stewart's main Spirit helpers, including...

- 'the passage of matter through matter', involving the 'unbreakable' plastic cable ties which hold Stewart's wrists to his arm chairs;

- physical contact, on numerous occasions, between Walter's ectoplasmic hand and the hand of the sitter - all visible in red light;

- Spirit people speaking without using the trumpet but using an 'independent' voice box - psychically built alongside Stewart by the Spirit scientists, and the most striking of all...

- Spirit people in solid form, with audible footsteps as they walk around the room, touching and conversing with the sitters.

Walter's avowed intention is to be able to illuminate such forms with their own Spirit lights, thus eliminating the need of a physical red light, which we used in our Home Circle in Middlesbrough. It must be remembered that a physical light of any kind or colour will always have, in varying degrees, an adverse effect on the phenomena, irrespective of the fact that permission has been given by the Spirit helpers. During the early periods of complete black-out, there are times when Stewart, who is strapped and roped into his chair, unexpectedly comes out of trance, to see the trumpets whirling in the air above him and hear Spirit voices through both the trumpet and the independent voice box - exactly the same as the renowned voice medium, Leslie Flint did. This is another splendid indication of the development his mediumship. The first time this happened in the Home Circle, Stewart was rather taken aback and made an excitable outburst such as − "What's that light flying around the room?" which created much laughter from the sitters who tried to explain to him that it was 'only' the trumpet's gyrations − a regular happening that they enjoyed each week - but it was totally new to Stewart. All good fun we would comment, by which time he was 'gone' again and the sitting would continue.

You will appreciate that this is not the appropriate place to write a biographical account of Stewart's remarkable mediumship. His brother Michael is far more competent in this respect, but my prime purpose is to let you know that the type of physical mediumship we experienced in the 1940's has not completely disappeared, but for personal reasons, is generally kept 'under wraps' in private Home Circles. Suffice for me to say that Stewart's public demonstrations started in 1992, mainly to help establish the newly-formed Noah's Ark Society which had been started in 1990, at the behest of Noah Zerdin from the Spirit world, to encourage physical psychic phenomena and support Home Circles which were sitting for such phenomena.

Stewart's extensive historical knowledge of this subject, supported by his huge library, made him ideally suited for the position of Archive Officer, which he held for many years in addition to his Presidency which he held later. His talks at the seminars were always interesting and informative, but his development as a physical medium was a matter of strict privacy - until he offered his services at the end of 1991. Colin Fry, then working under the name of 'Lincoln', was already giving public demonstrations at the seminars, so Stewart, finally overcoming his nervousness and foregoing his privacy, delighted the membership with his excellent mediumship.

As the saying goes... 'the rest is history', and he has given scores of outstanding demonstrations throughout the United Kingdom and overseas, but remains a very quiet and private man who is deeply committed to his weekly Home Circle, where Walter Stinson and the Spirit scientists carry out their experiments - which Ann and I have been delighted to be involved with.

Another important aspect of Home Circles is the regularity of the sittings, irrespective of whether all members are available. There are normally eight sitters in Stewart's Home Circle, but because of holidays and work commitments the numbers may sometimes be reduced - as was the case on 30th January 1996 when my recorded notes show that we had a remarkable sitting with only three sitters, Denise, Ann and myself, in addition to Stewart of course. Walter Stinson soon controlled Stewart saying: "There are certain experiments we would like to try (my comments 'with just four of us?') - what we lose in numbers we more than make up for in harmony....of course it would be nice to see a full circle but we understand and thank you few folks for coming to allow us this evening to push forward with our developments ..... we hope you will have something to take away with you to make the others envious (much laughter) - no promises, but we'll see."

After a few more minutes talking, Walter then left and was quickly followed by a very clear, cultured lady's voice, who explained she attended all our meetings but had been waiting in the wings for a long time, with great patience, to be given the opportunity to try to speak to us. She explained that the content of her talk tonight was much less important than the quality of her actual speech during this 'her maiden speech' and would identify herself when she felt more confident. She continued to speak very clearly, thanked us for welcoming her and listening to her for these few moments. That proved to be the introduction to a lady who soon became, and remains an important member of the Spirit team - friendly Freda Johnson.

Within a minute of the lady leaving, a gentleman spoke - with some difficulty at first, but he soon improved and talked in an intelligent manner. "I'm bound to ask - where is everybody this evening?" We explained about holidays and work and his following comments, I feel, are worthy of note. "All that really matters is that you should come together each week, that you should continue the contact. I find this quite amazing myself....quite amazing that I in a world removed from yours can make myself heard in your world...and what is even more surprising is that I can hear you speaking also....There is so much being done actually....with the mediumship....with the circle....we are as you say in your world, pushing the boat out ....stretching forward....reaching forward....continuously trying to broaden our horizons. It is only in that way can that we can accomplish all we hope to in time. Nothing was ever gained by satisfaction at what has so far been achieved....things can only be developed further by pushing all the time, continuously within safety limits of course....that goes without saying. There are many souls surrounding you tonight, standing behind you, Mr Harrison, it is not my task to pass on messages but there is a Minnie with you....she is so insistent" (thank you, my mother).

Christopher immediately followed, complaining that he had been unable to get in, there were so many others wanting to come. He asked me if I knew the name Tom Tompkinson (yes, an old friend of Sydney Shipman) and who was Mrs Lumsden, and did Doris (my late wife) know her (yes, she was Doris's granny). All three of us then felt Spirit people touching us from behind - Denise being tapped on her arm, which we could clearly hear; I felt someone touching my head very gently; Ann heard someone walking towards her blowing gently, followed by someone gently touching her head and then a firm hand on each of her shoulders, pressing down very strongly. The bell which had been kicked on the floor was then up and ringing in front of us and was finally dropped on to Denise's knee, along with the writing pad and the pencil, which is always put at the side of Stewart. On more than one occasion we heard Stewart's chair being lifted and thumped on the floor, and I suddenly felt the ropes, which had been alongside Stewart drop on to my knees.

Christopher then asked to try a book test with me, which proved very informative. He briefly described the cover of the book and I had to read page 14, which had a crease on it. From his description I soon found the book, an old paper backed Lyceum Education handbook which I used regularly as a lad, turned to page 14, which did have a crease across the middle and found only nine lines at the top of the page, which I now quote –

"One of the most striking features of regularly held Home Circles is the unfailing punctuality of the Spirit guests. They never forget their appointment with us. Spirit return then is so

natural that it has always happened and always will happen, so long as love and friendship are found in the universe. Just so long will those who have crossed the bridge of death into Spirit life desire to prove that love and friendship are of the Spirit and can never die".

I felt this was so apt considering what we had previously been told earlier in this sitting.

At the end of the sitting when we switched on the light, we saw our shoes, which we always remove during a sitting, had been moved around the room and more importantly, written on the pad on Denise's knee was - "Denise, Love, G.O.L.." - a message from Gladys Osborne Leonard who is wanting to work through Denise when the time is opportune. A wonderful hour's sitting, with only four sitters instead of the usual eight. To those who are sitting in their own Home Circles:- keep the continuity of sitting irrespective of the number of sitters - you owe it to your Spirit workers.

The mention of the book test reminded me of the Transatlantic Experiment on 1st November 1994 held on each side of the Atlantic, at the same hour (allowing for time zone differences). It was proposed by Riley Heagerty who resided in Oswego, New York, U.S.A.. Riley wrote to Stewart to see if Stewart's Spirit controls could interlock with his vibration in his home, from a lock of hair and a small picture of himself, which he had sent to Stewart. My personal interest in this experiment concerns the fact that I had sat with Stewart the week before, which was the original date fixed for the experiment, but for various reasons it had to be delayed, so I was not present and had no effect on, the 'happenings'. A detailed report is included in Katie Halliwell's well-written booklet about 'Trance and Physical Mediumship Experiences' linked with Stewart's Circle, but I would like to refer to one significant piece of evidence given through Christopher. In Riley's own words, when he commented after listening to the tape recording made during the sitting in Hull......

"Let's move on to Christopher's input - 'a big bookcase lots and lots of books' - perfectly correct of course. 'Third shelf down, fourteenth book in from the left ....indeed a pamphlet ...next to this pamphlet is a book and the cover is torn'. The pamphlet of all things my friends is 'Visits by Our Friends from the Other Side', about Minnie Harrison, written by Tom Harrison, and next to the pamphlet is a book with torn cover - 'Wisdom of the Gods' by Denis Bradley. Stewart mentioned that Mr Harrison might be a guest sitter. I don't know if he was, but either way it was astonishing."

Just another example of how very close our Spirit friends can get, when called upon with love and harmony.

Katie Halliwell has been sitting fairly regularly with Stewart since 1999, primarily to collect information for her booklet and audio tapes about Stewart's Circle entitled 'Experiences of Trance and Physical Mediumship', due for release in October 2003. She has been profoundly deaf since birth, but because her speech is quite normal people do not realise how deaf she is. She attended speech therapy sessions throughout her schooldays at the Odsal House School for the Deaf in Bradford.

Let Katie continue: - "Back in 1999 and 2000, Freda, knowing about my hearing deficiency, would often comment to the other sitters...'Has Katie heard me?' As I was sitting in total darkness I was unable to use my other sense to help me cope. I was unable to lip read, unable to watch people's facial expressions, unable to look for signs that somebody was talking to me, but I was never left out. The Spirit people and Circle members always did their utmost to help me communicate with the Other Side.

"When I read Ann's transcript of my tapes, only then did I realise how many words I did not pick up during those first two years. But since the 'special conditions' were prepared for me by the Spirit helpers, Freda and Walter no longer have constantly to ask the Circle to ask me whether I have heard them. Although I am sometimes slow to respond and still need to use my hearing aids, I now have no difficulty receiving oral communication from the Spirit World.

"At home, listening to the tapes, I have to concentrate on the words - but in the séance room I don't seem to have this problem. There is an element of clarity and because I don't have to concentrate so hard, I can join in the conversation. I have also noticed that when I go into the room I always feel as if I am wearing some kind of hat. There is definitely a light pressure on and around my head and ears, with a strong tingling sensation above and around the head.

"With these 'special conditions', the only time the Circle had to interpret for me was when John Sloan spoke to me in his broad Scottish accent. This wasn't a hearing problem - just that I could not understand what he was saying!" Katie was not the only one!

During a sitting on 4th May 2000, Walter expressed his sincere wish to Katie that "We in our world would like nothing better than we should be able to cure that which is wrong - but that is not so - it is not possible. We can do what we can, but where you have lost in one direction you have gained so much in another. (K: Yes, definitely) You are a dear soul. You may feel you are a voice in the wilderness - but let me tell you, you are beloved of my world. Your words, whether spoken or written, carry such import and will affect the minds and hearts of more people than you can begin to imagine. Your love for our world is recognised in our world."

Then on 9th April 2002, a Spirit voice was heard via the Independent Voice, saying that the speaking mechanism had been well established and constructed that evening. "We are aware of your hearing impediment Katie, and have done all that we can to construct speaking tubes from your left and right ears. We are uncertain how long we shall be able to maintain them but shall do our best." Similar comments were made on 27th August, with the Independent Voice speaker adding…"The first part of your work is now almost complete. We know that through your efforts, through your love for my world, your love for this great and wondrous Truth, many people will be touched by your words, will be touched by all you have done and therefore it will bring great comfort."

Then during our Sitting on 19th August 2003, Walter Stinson made a special request concerning Katie's situation. Quote: "Tom, Ann, - it may be of interest to point out to you both, that which is so obvious but which you may have failed to appreciate. We say this because, in the work you are involved in at present - your memoirs Tom, this will, deservedly so, demand a place within.

"You know that our friend Katie is in many ways profoundly deaf. When she comes within this room, where our two worlds meet and blend together, then - because of the work she has done and will perform, it is vitally important and necessary to ensure that the lady would be able to hear all that transpires. For that reason, the scientific people in my world connected with this Circle, began to work upon a method by which, once she was here within, and the light had been extinguished, arrangements could be made so that she would miss nothing and would be able to hear. Is that not so Katie? (K: It is Walter).

"That in itself again demonstrates quite clearly the power of the Spirit. Do you understand Tom? (T: I do) The power of the Spirit - so we say to all those folks who may have impediments of hearing, that within our room, arrangements will always be made to try to ensure that those who are so afflicted will be able to appreciate and understand and hear for themselves. We know that there are so many within your world with no understanding of our work, who will always advance theories, no matter how ridiculous they may be, no matter how inappropriate, to account for what takes place here. But let them explain that Tom. Hmm?"

Ann and I have been, and still are, privileged to enjoy and witness a superabundance of such genuine physical phenomena through such a humble, self-effacing, friendly medium and I will let Ann describe some of her unique experiences concerning Ectoplasm and fully materialised Spirit people walking around the Circle room.

"While I was transcribing the tape for Katie I was so pleased to hear Freda's description of what ectoplasm is. She gave the following description "Life itself is a trinity. There is the physical body, the spiritual body and there is the mind. Within your spiritual body is your mind. The physical brain gives expression to your mind. Understand therefore that there is physical matter and there is spiritual matter. Between the two is a form of dynamic energy, which we often refer to as 'ectoplasm' for it is neither physical nor spiritual in nature. It lies between the two states. It is both spiritual and physical. When we attempt to manifest in a physical manner we must take from the medium the vital energy, ectoplasm. Ectoplasm can be manipulated by the scientific people in my world in such a manner that its molecular structure can be changed from something that is almost smoke-like in appearance to something, which is solid to the touch. I make it sound very simple….. but it is very complex and that is why ectoplasm is extremely sensitive to any form of light…"

This 'change of molecular structure' was demonstrated to me in August 1998 when, due to Gaynor's absence, I was able to sit next to Stewart in the Home Circle. We had already had several Spirit visitors when Freda returned and asked us to test the red light under the surface of the table so that they could try out the brightness that the ectoplasm could withstand that night. As the ectoplasm was extracted, via Stewart's navel we were told, we could hear it fizzing and crackling and Michael joked about it being the cheesecloth that mediums are supposed to secrete to produce the 'apparitions'. I commented it sounded more like crinkly cellophane and Tom told us that it was just as he remembered 50 years before. That evening we were able to turn the light up higher than ever before and see the amorphous shape of the ectoplasm, in silhouette, against the light. It was then formed into a pincer with which a 'trumpet' or other objects could have been picked up.

Freda then told us to turn the light out and asked me for my hand, but to turn it palm up. I held out my right hand towards Stewart. My wrist was grasped by strong fingers so that I could not move it out of the position they wanted. Stewart, as usual, was fastened into his chair with ropes, and his arms secured to the arms of his chair with strong cable ties so it could not have been his hand grasping my wrist. I felt something moving across my fingers. In texture it was like a small plastic bag full of liquid. The 'bag' was moved up and down across my fingers and then suddenly it was gone and my wrist was released. I replaced my hand on my knee.

Freda requested "Again Ann." I held out my hand and again, fingers grasped my wrist. This time a piece of thin but roughish 'cloth' was draped and pulled across my fingers. I told the others "It's lying across my hand. It's like cloth." Immediately the response came from Freda: "Like cheesecloth." Yes it was! It was quite different from a previous sitting when it had felt like silk voile. As quickly as it had come, it had gone. Freda spoke again, "Then let us try in what, I suppose, would be described as its dematerialised state. That is to say the state before it takes on a solid form. Give me your hand again, Ann. You must tell everyone here if you are able to feel anything. I am taking your hand with my other hand."

This time when I put out my hand, as well as being held around the wrist, other fingers grasped the tips of my fingers. There was a slight regurgitating sound from Stewart, and then across my hand came a cool draught. So gently, a beautiful cool breeze flowing across my hand. The feeling is difficult to describe because it was nothing like someone blowing on your hand, but more like the cold air that flows on to you when you open the freezer. It continued for some seconds before I became aware that the coolness was decreasing and the 'breeze' was becoming quite warm. My fingers were released and I lowered my arm.

Once again I had been honoured. They had given me the chance to experience what so few people have the chance of - to know the feel of that most rare substance - ectoplasm. I had previously felt it as flesh when Walter invited me to feel the back of his hand when he materialised it against the under-lit table. But to be trusted and loved enough to be given that evening's unique experience is humbling and carries a responsibility. I have been given these wonderful 'close encounters' because of the contact I have with people when Tom gives his talks, to pass on how near our Spirit friends really are, and what is possible between us when there is love, harmony and dedication.

All the members of the circle experience other wonderful close encounters. One evening when Gaynor was decidedly 'under the weather' and waiting for hospital treatment, she was instructed to relax. She felt two hands upon her head and experienced a deep sense of peace and healing. As the materialised forms have increased the distance they can come away from the medium, those of us at the far side of the room have felt their hands and frequently now, more than two hands are materialised, touching different people at the same time. One instance, again in the tape transcribed for Katie, which is available with her book, you can hear the conversation as Katie and Mike have hands touching them simultaneously. A number of times June and Gaynor, sitting more than six feet from each other, have described hands being placed on their heads and playing with their hair. I have felt large hands, but Gaynor has felt small child-like hands.

The hands are not only placed on our heads. I have had my hand picked up from my lap, slapped sharply, to show how solid *they* are, and then kissed. This is all done, unerringly, in complete darkness. They may hold your shoulder, tweak an ear and stroke your cheek, as happened to Tom when his mother returned one evening. But we are not the only beneficiaries of these encounters. One evening, having been told to keep perfectly still, the materialised form standing in front of me (I know he was there because of the energy which was almost tangible) placed his very large hands on my head and while moving his fingers through my hair, which is very wavy, remarked what a strange sensation it was for him to feel my hair."

Thank you, Katie and Ann, for your input.

All this takes place in total darkness as yet, but when we sat in August 2003 Walter Stinson held a ball of green spirit light in one hand and put his other hand close to the light so that Ann and I could see it quite clearly. We could also see the fingers of the hand holding the light silhouetted against the ball as he held it. Their determination to prove to the world that not only do they exist but they are so close, pushes the experimentation on and on, but always within safe limits for the medium and all of the sitters.

I am convinced there is so much more yet to come with the combined efforts of Walter, Christopher, Freda and above all, of course, of Stewart and his lifelong doorkeeper White Feather with the host of backroom Spirit workers. A truly formidable and resolute team.

It makes you think!

In Stewart Alexander's séances his knees are marked with strips of luminous tape secured by a length of sellotape. In Home Circle sittings in 1995, while the Spirit scientists were experimenting, the tabs would be removed by the spirits and thrown through the air or attached to some other object away from the medium. On one occasion, in May '95, one was attached to my trumpet, which was being used in the circle. I decided that it should stay on as an extra marker, covering it with more sellotape to fix it firmly to the surface, as the original tape was crumpled.

During a Noah's Ark 'public' sitting on a very hot July night in Rotherham Ann noticed that that extra tab had gone although it had been there before the start of the evening.

On Monday 5th February 1996 I brought my book of road maps in from the car and we discovered the first pages, well into the centre of the pages, were stuck together with tape and on prising them open there was the luminous strip and its crumpled tape. How had it got there we have no physical explanation. The trumpet was always carried in a zipped cloth bag. At no time had the trumpet and maps been in contact in the car but if they had been in contact the tab was too securely fixed to have accidentally transferred itself; especially into the centre of an inside page of the book!

I think they were having fun and just showing us how close they are. We still have the piece of tape in our memorabilia.

25

Our Home Circles in the 1990s

The bulk of my book has been concerned with our Middlesbrough Home Circle in the late 1940's and 1950's but it is important to let you know that similar physical phenomena is still occurring in Home Circles. In addition to Stewart Alexander's Circle, Ann and I were members of two Home Circles, one in our friends' home about an hour's drive away, from May 1994 to 1997, which was followed by one in our own home in Brayton near Selby from January 1998 until we moved to Spain in January 2000.

In January 1998, when Ann and I had moved to Brayton, near Selby, we were fortunate to have our two friends from the old circle join us in our own Home Circle. The format was very similar with our female friend being the main medium, although each of us, in turn, sat to develop our own mediumship. I made a 'cabinet' of black curtains on a hoop of wood, which I hoped would meet with approval. When I sat in it for the first time, on a swivel chair, the main control of the circle spun my chair around quickly. I caught against the curtains and wrecked the whole contraption. Obviously something stronger was needed and as they explained – 'material that will hold the energy', so for our Circle I made a structured cabinet with three sides made from sheets of plywood painted black, and the front having a black curtain on a draw rail. This one met with the approval of our Spirit friends, who told us it helped to concentrate the psychic energy for whoever was sitting in it and we all felt it when we had our turns in the cabinet. We were delighted to welcome our friend's Spirit Guide again, and also the 'rough diamond', who was his old cheery self.

We were again often to have a fully materialised Spirit person standing in front of the cabinet curtain while the medium was seated inside. To prove to us that it was not the Medium standing there, occasionally they would rap the body all the way up from knee height to the top of the head to show it was a complete body, and when we asked if that was the medium, the trumpet would indicate 'no' by moving left to right, like a shake of the head, and then tap the top of the medium's head inside the cabinet. We always left a writing pad and pencil on the small table in the centre of the Circle and often found printed messages from the Spirit Guide when the light was switched on.

Our weekly sittings were so joyful and friendly, taking me back to our days with the Saturday Night Club 50 years before. We had occasional guest sitters including our friends Carol and Hazel, but the sitting on Saturday 20th November 1999, shortly before our move to Spain, was particularly interesting when our very good friend, Eric, was our guest.

Ann and I first met Eric and his wife Jackie at a Lodge Christmas Social in 1997. Some years previously Eric had been a year away from being in the Chair at our Lodge, but had had to step down because of heart problems. To keep himself involved he had become Social secretary and had therefore been responsible for arranging the social. The wife of one of the other members, who was sitting next to Eric, mentioned to him that she was a 'spiritual healer' and had this urge to put her hand on his knee for healing. As Eric commented - what a chat up line! - but he was quite sure that Marjorie did not know he was recovering from a serious tendon operation. Marjorie had then told him that he ought to contact us and later introduced us to each other. So that was Eric's introduction to 'Spiritual and Psychic' matters, particularly the healing aspect, and this is what he later wrote..…

"My first visit to Brayton was to take a friend for healing. Philip had terminal lung cancer but was keen to come. We both had healing that day and I remember Philip commenting on the return journey that the experience had been very calming and peaceful for him. I had relaxed visibly during my session and appeared to be almost in a trance state. Due to pressure of work and Philip's later inability to travel, I was unable to take him again and he died in the April. His widow later told me that he had died peacefully, and felt sure that the one visit to Brayton had given him inner strength.

"It seems inexplicable now, but almost a year went by before I visited Tom and Ann again. We met at Ladies' Night in February 1999, by which time I was recovering from a triple bypass operation. This time however, my concern was for a relative who was seriously ill and I asked if they could pass healing thoughts to help him. I was invited to visit them the following week for a healing session for both of us. As this first healing session was drawing to a close I was amazed to be suddenly aware of my relative kneeling in front of me. Unfortunately, as with Philip, it had proved too late for him, but it started a regular meeting for me with Tom and Ann, initially to give me strength to help with my recovery.

"From the beginning Tom said he was aware of an old lady's presence, who was a relative but not my grandmother. It soon became clear that this was indeed my great Aunt Florrie who lived with us and to whom I had become very close. He then became aware of a man standing with his hands clasped in front of him - like a minister. At that time Tom did not know Jackie's father was a Church of England vicar who had died two years previously. He was subsequently joined by someone of a higher rank than Jackie's dad, who turned out to be her 'Uncle John', the Bishop of Sheffield, a family friend who officiated at our wedding. When I returned home from this visit, a photograph of Jackie's dad had fallen off the wall, and during the evening the curtains fluttered for some minutes as though there was a 'presence'.

Over the following months we had some very powerful sessions and Tom became aware of a crowd, all trying to get in, with Philip joining the aforementioned Spirits. It became obvious during the year that all was not well with my heart and a second operation was scheduled for 10th December. I visited Tom and Ann very regularly to build up the extra energy to help me through the operation. They had talked to me about their sittings with their friend the medium and her husband and felt I must join them one Saturday evening. I had always declined as I did not feel up to driving on my own in an evening, and did not want to infringe on Jackie's weekend as she worked all week. They said if she did not want to join us they would quite understand and she could bring a book and read in the study - which was what was arranged.

"I did not know what to expect and when I saw the cabinet, trumpet, bells and notebook and pencil I must admit I wondered what was coming. We started with songs and carols and I joined in with gusto. Within seconds the trumpet was flying all round the room and we had a number of visitations including one of the medium's Spirit helpers, who spoke to me directly and took a long time to explain that his job was to receive new Spirits - and he assured me all would be well. I remember saying to Tom afterwards that I was concerned that the communicator had gone to such great lengths to tell me about his job as 'Spiritual receptionist' and hoped he wasn't just preparing me! This was said with tongue in cheek but the communicator assured Tom at a subsequent sitting, that he just wanted to put me at my ease and apologised - which of course I accepted."

The week before Eric came to the Saturday sitting, we had agreed, on request from one of our Spirit friends, a delightful little girl, to put a few jelly babies in a dish for the Spirit children the following week. Ann therefore put five in a dish and put them on the table in the centre of the Circle, which Eric saw before we started. The medium's Spirit Guide spoke to Eric as soon we opened: "Good evening Eric. I want to say before proceeding any further, you are perfectly safe, don't worry and your good lady is safe also. Now sing." During the singing our heavy brass crinoline lady bell was picked up and rung above our heads, which amazed Eric. The trumpet was also rapidly moved around the room before finally stopping in mid-air in front of the cabinet, pointing towards Eric. We heard a faint voice trying to speak to him and eventually heard "This is Auntie" who then briefly spoke to him.

This proved to be excellent evidence for Eric, which he later explained to us. During our previous healing sessions with him, I often felt the strong presence of a lady and from the description I gave him he recognised her as one of his relatives, 'Auntie Florrie'. She was in fact his mother's Aunt but had become very close to Eric and frequently took him on day trips. What we had not known, however, was that as the 'senior' Aunt in the family, she was known to everyone within the family simply as 'Auntie' - without the Florrie, which was only used when talking to other people, like ourselves.

The Spirit child came again to thank Ann for the jelly babies and said they hadn't been to eat them all, which rather puzzled us at the time. When the light was switched on at the end of the sitting however, there on the dish, which had had five jelly babies when we started, was only half a black one, which, from its appearance, looked as though it had been bitten through! We were all quite surprised by this - especially Eric of course, and we still have it, wrapped, in our box of memorabilia. Eric had been enjoyably perplexed by it all and was delighted to see that the Spirit Guide had printed a message for him on the pad which read: "We are with you always." This page was torn out for Eric to keep as a memento of his first sitting in a Home Circle. And his account   finishes with…"This was an evening I will never forget."

We became very good friends with Eric and Jackie and did all we could to help Eric through his second, more serious, operation. It seemingly worked as Eric wrote…"I was certainly aware of the help that Tom and Ann were giving me. Before the first operation I was terrified, but this time, although I knew what to expect, and that it would be more serious than the previous one, I was relaxed and laid back. In the event the operation was much more difficult. I was on the operating table for five and a half hours where they performed a quadruple bypass and reconstruction of an artery.

The Spirits were right - I did have a rough recovery with additional pain and numerous setbacks including a transfusion of the wrong blood. My kidneys almost failed and I was hours away from dialysis. Tom and Ann played a major part in helping me through this, visiting the hospital in Hull and I always felt a boost when I needed it most. I have to say on a very selfish note however, that I considered their move to Spain in January 2000, most inopportune! Since then we have visited each other and had weekly 'remote' healing sessions, which Tom likes to call 'energy balancing'. These have certainly helped and have become stronger over the months. Thank you Tom and Ann, I could not have managed without you."

As I have said, we are very close friends and are delighted to know that we have been the means of allowing our Spirit friends and helpers to help Eric so much in such times of need.

During this period we were invited to sit from time to time with a Circle near Doncaster. Kate had written to me for advice following my talk in Rotherham. She was developing as a deep trance and transfiguration medium and we were delighted to have the opportunity to help her. Through Kate I was introduced to a new Spirit companion who wanted to work with me for healing. Known as Ching-Lee, he identifies himself by rubbing my hands along my arms as though in wide sleeved Chinese robes. A few days later he spoke to me again through another reputable trance medium at the Arthur Findlay College and then, to confirm his identity, a short time later, I was given a psychic portrait by a medium in South Wales. It was good to have that first contact through Kate and he still works with me. We enjoyed many sittings both at Kate's and our home in Brayton. Thank you both for your devotion to the world of Spirit.

Our last Saturday sitting in Brayton before our emigration to Spain was full of the usual joyful activity. Our medium was controlled, but we were told her Spirit Guide would not be speaking as he was busy with something special. We had a most enjoyable sitting and during the circle Ann and I felt something fly past our shoulders and drop behind us near our fireplace. We thought it was probably the notebook, which had been placed on the table as normal, but we were in for a big surprise. When we switched on the light Ann looked behind us and saw a white envelope lying on the floor. She picked it up and commented that it was addressed to Mr and Mrs Harrison.

Our medium quickly leaned across and took it from Ann's hand saying it was hers and we weren't suppose to have it until they were leaving - it contained a card wishing us well in our new home in Eagles' Nest, the small urbanisation in which we are still living. She was obviously quite puzzled as she had left it, with a similar one from their daughter, in her handbag outside the room, in the hallway on the foot of the stairs.

The door to the hallway was completely sealed with a curtain, which had been fixed with drawing pins when we were all inside the room. So her Spirit Guide must have de-materialised it, moved it from inside her zipped handbag, brought it into the Circle room and to our great joy had also printed his initials on the front of the envelope - at the same time leaving their daughter's card still in the handbag. They had signed the card from the two of them, but her Spirit Guide had no intention of being left out! He had certainly had a busy evening and we treasure the card and envelope, which is on a bookshelf in our library, a very special, tangible memory of two remarkable Home Circles. We wish to record our sincere and loving thanks to our earthly friends, their wonderful Spirit Guide and all the devoted Spirit team who gave so much joy to so many people.

Since being in Spain, we have continued the weekly 'distant healing' sessions, not only for Eric, but for many others whom we know are in need of such help and have recently started another home circle in our own home. We are currently living near the coast in the Costa Blanca area and are delighted to find so many interested 'extranjeros' along this coastal strip. There are at least four Spiritual Centres within a few kilometres of Torrevieja and others are being considered further north. Ray and June Smith continue the work near Gibraltar and Frederick and Valerie Smith likewise on the Algarve coast near Faro. It would seem as though the psychic energy down this strip of the Iberian coast is developing into quite a 'powerhouse' to be used for the benefit of mankind. Long may it thrive!

26

Life in the Spirit World

"*What is it really like?*"

This is a question I am frequently asked about the Spirit World and I have had many instances where our Spirit friends have told us about life in their world. We are assured that, once they have adjusted after their transition, and in many cases, a recovery or recuperation period, they all live very full lives in whatever style or fashion they wish. They have told us that at the time of transition, no one is alone. There is always someone to meet us, often a close relative or loved one, but not necessarily so.

During one of her visits Aunt Agg sat on the chair that my mother had vacated when she moved into the cabinet, and described what had happened in her case. It was February 1942 and they had just finished lunch in their home in Cricklewood. Aunt Agg was getting ready to travel into London to demonstrate her mediumship at a meeting in one of the large public halls, either the Queen's or Aeolian. These meetings were very popular during World War Two, with crowds of up to 2,500.

She suddenly felt a severe pain in her head and sat down to recover. The pain proved to be a fatal brain haemorrhage. She said she remembered nothing after sitting down until finding herself sitting on a bench in a beautiful park - full of so many different trees, bushes, flowers and plants of colours she did not recognize. They were so bright and pristine and shone in what appeared to be brilliant sunshine, although there was no sun to be seen. Everything was so calm and peaceful like a summer's afternoon - but even more so, and she found it very difficult to describe the overall picture.

Her first thoughts, sitting on the bench, were... "What am I doing here - I should be in London taking the meeting," and she felt rather puzzled by it all. There seemed to be no one else around except for a lady in the distance walking in her direction. She was intrigued as the lady approached her and finally stood alongside, smiling at her. "Hello" said Aunt Agg, "I seem to know you but just can't place you." The lady then explained why Aunt Agg seemed to know her - she was one of Aunt Agg's band of Spirit helpers and had been chosen to welcome her into the Spirit World. She invited Aunt Agg to accompany her through this beautiful park and she would take her to meet her own family and loved ones who were awaiting her arrival. All so tranquil and pleasurable, as would be expected for someone so deeply involved for so many years.

Sam Hildred's story was slightly different when he passed over suddenly through a heart attack on Christmas Day 1945. He told us that he wakened up in a bed in what seemed like an open-air hospital with all the brightness that Aunt Agg described. It was not painful or difficult - just like waking from a sleep when on the earth. Some of his close family were at the bedside and everyone was very helpful. His slight knowledge of life after death, through his visit to Helen Duncan's materialization Circle with Sydney in 1938, had helped him tremendously - in the same way as Jack Graham had told us that it had helped him, although his introduction to the Spirit World at our Home Circle was only a week before his passing. Length of time is unimportant - so long as the individual has an open mind and is willing to accept even the possibility of a continuous life.

The lack of knowledge of a life after death, in most cases, is not a stumbling block and most people just find themselves there, expecting to be in Heaven, with Jesus perhaps, but a negative attitude or religiously constricted outlook could well have an adverse effect when transition to the Spirit World occurs. This was clearly demonstrated in the case of our neighbour, Mr Matheson, who, because of his very strict religious upbringing, believed that there was absolutely nothing after death and was completely confused and frustrated by his new surroundings. According to our mutual friend, Jack Graham, who had passed to the Spirit World a few months earlier, it was almost a year, in our time, before he was able to convince Mr M. of the truth of life after death, thus freeing him from his frustration and confusion.

We also witnessed in our Home Circle another similar incident, but for a completely different reason, concerning Sydney's Uncle Dick, who had been crippled with arthritis for years before his passing. He was not religiously bigoted, but unfortunately knew nothing about the Spirit World. Sydney made enquiries about his uncle when his father spoke to him from the Spirit World. He was sad to hear that his uncle just 'sat in a corner' on his chair still unable to move because of the arthritis which he believed was still restricting his movements.

His father said he was trying to help him understand his new environment and that the old physical body had now gone, but many months passed before the uncle himself, actually materialized, came out of the cabinet and held out his arms towards Sydney, expressing his great delight that it had now 'all gone!' If only he had been aware of the Truth of life after death before his transition, he would not have had to suffer that extra incapacity.

It is so true that here on earth we are creatures of conditioning, both mental and physical, and such cases do occur, but the majority of people have no difficulty whatsoever with the transition. With the help of their loved ones who are already over there, they soon settle down into the new environment. They tell us they thoroughly enjoy a life unhindered by the restrictions of a physical body, especially where that body had become a useless shell - racked with disease causing untold pain. More importantly, not one of them ever said they wanted to return permanently to life on the earth. They were always extremely happy to visit us and pass on their messages of love, but were adamant that life in the Spirit World was so much better and they were patiently waiting for the time when their loved ones would join them.

I well remember during one of my mother's trance sittings, an elderly lady Spirit visitor who had no knowledge of Spiritualism, was having great difficulty in speaking through my mother. However, with the help and encouragement of her grandson, one of our guests that night, she finally managed to say a few words to him. Her first words, with great apprehension, in a rather croaky voice were: "Am I back on the earth then?" As we affirmed that was so, she hastily added in a very anxious voice, "But I'll be able to go back won't I?" We immediately assured her she could and indeed would go back, at which her tone and demeanour quickly became much more relaxed and she had a good few minutes chat with her grandson, Wilf.

As much as she had wanted to talk to Wilf, the question of being able 'to go back' had been of paramount importance to her, a very strong indication that her life in the Spirit World was the 'real' one for her.

Aunt Agg reminded us, however, that as good as life is in the Spirit World, we must live our lives here to the best of our abilities until it is our allotted time to go - overcoming the difficulties which confront us and, especially, learning the lessons of friendliness and fellowship which are so important over there. Suicide cases are very troubled souls, she said, needing so much help and guidance and she often thanked us for the way we were able to assist them during our sittings that created so much radiant energy for them to use.

We understand that the Spirit World is very much a counterpart to this world, with Spirits of all ages at different levels of development. Our memory goes with us when we pass over as it is part of our Spirit body, so we can converse about matters relating to the earth, and our friends on the earth will recognize us by what we say, just as happens on the telephone here although we cannot see each other. We will meet people of similar character and outlook, which will decide where we shall live and from which level we will start our progress. It is all a question of mental un-foldment and development. They told us that our position and condition when we enter the Spirit World depends greatly on how we live our lives here - and as we sow, so shall we reap.

There are of course, the dark regions which are inhabited by the sinister, unkind or materialistic people who have not led amiable, friendly or helpful lives on the earth, and it is only by their own efforts can they progress to the brighter regions. We were told of certain groups of advanced Spirits called the White Brotherhood who work in these regions to educate and enlighten those dwelling there. They are certainly not left alone to suffer indefinitely but they have to show genuine remorse and a desire to redress the wrongdoings of the past. For some it may be a very slow process but at least they are always given the opportunity. Stephen Turoff's book 'Seven Steps to Eternity' covers numerous instances of such cases and is well worth reading, as is the 'Wheel of Eternity' by Helen Greaves.

Those who pass over as babies or young children need to be cared for, cherished, loved, nurtured and taught the lessons of life, but in a much more enlightened manner than here. Mona Hildred, Gladys' sister and one of our regular Spirit visitors, had passed over as a girl of 12.

She explained to us how she had been cared for in a group of children before being given the responsibility to act as guardian to Prudence, a lovely young Spirit, who had recently passed over as a baby. She always brought her to our sittings, to help her understand and appreciate life here and enjoy the company of our regular Spirit-children visitors. From time to time, such young children are taken back to their earthly homes to maintain close family contact and we understand that the mothers in particular often 'sense' they are there - a joy for both sides.

During question time after my talks, the question about '*age*' in the Spirit World is a regular 'chestnut'. Do babies and young children grow up? Do elderly people continue to get older? Or do we stay the same as when we pass over? The simple answer is that 'age', as such, applies only to the physical body, which is incorporated in our solar time scale.

Whilst on this earth, it is only the physical body which ages and not the Spirit within. The Spirit develops and 'matures', and continues to mature in the Spirit World according to the desires and preferences of the individual. The Spirits of babies and young children certainly continue to develop into maturity under the guidance and tuition of loving carers, such as Mona, and become responsible for their own development along with their peers and friends.

After giving this brief explanation I would then ask members of the audience to raise their hands if, they felt, they were older than 39 years. This always created much laughter but the response was always the same at each meeting - no more than two or three hands would be raised and these were soon dropped when the real impact of my question became apparent - not if they *were* older than 39, but only if, in the mind, they *felt* it. Is it not true that mentally we all feel so much younger than the years on the calendar - whether it be 39 or even less, like my wife who says she is not more than 29?

So often do we find the saying - "The spirit is willing but the body is weak!" applying in our senior years here; but not so in the Spirit World where the Spirit is in complete control and elderly people may in fact, revert to their 'prime' in looks, continuing then to mature in mind. It is only when they 'return', through a medium or Home Circle, do they show themselves as we would remember them.

Dedicated doctors and nurses can still pursue their calling in the Spirit World in a variety of ways. People who pass over after long and debilitating illnesses do not suddenly recover and become completely well again. Although they have lost the useless physical body, the Spirit body and the mind are still in need of caring, healing skills, often for some period of time.

Large scale accidents and catastrophes need rescue teams from the Spirit side, as well as from here, to help both those who have passed over and those still critically ill. On many occasions during our sittings Sunrise would tell us that certain of our regular Spirit visitors were not present because they had been called to help in an emergency. Such is the close link between the two worlds. Whilst they do not have the means to avert such tragedies, our Spirit friends are always there to meet and comfort those who have passed over.

Whilst 'solar time' may not apply to life in the Spirit World, there are those who still have close sentimental links with people on the earth and still 'keep an eye' on our clocks. Like some husbands and wives, parents and grandparents, there are Spirit companions and helpers who choose to remain in close contact with the earth's vibrations so that their loving presence may continue to be felt, especially in times of need and often anniversaries.

A very good friend of ours, who has only recently become interested in these matters, told me that as he lay in bed one morning, he suddenly became aware of a host of relatives and friends from the Spirit World surrounding his bed. He said they were all smiling and seemed very happy. He told his wife when she returned home in the evening, but said he was puzzled why they had been there. She quickly told him the reason - it was his birthday, but he had not connected their presence with that fact in the morning.

Some without such close links may wish to improve their knowledge of the Spirit World and perhaps move into a higher vibration, not so dissimilar in structure to our education through primary schools, secondary schools, colleges and universities. We all have freedom of choice to live the kind of life we desire without the material restrictions of earthly life. One of our Spirit visitors in a recent trance Circle we were members of, told us that part of his work was to meet individuals who, like him, knew nothing about the Spirit World, and explain to them what their transition had meant. Furthermore, he said, he was learning to play the piano - one of his unattained ambitions on earth.

Some months later he came again to tell us he had stopped his piano lessons because, he very proudly announced, he had been 'promoted'. He had done so well in his other work he had been asked to move to a higher vibration and show people how they could begin to progress, so he was concentrating very much on this new work. He might go back to the piano lessons later. He was so pleased that he could do something to help other people like himself who knew nothing about the life after death. When on earth, he had considered himself a bit of a rough diamond who, with his wife, ran a public house in Birmingham, but this had proved to be no drawback whatsoever to the development of his Spirit and we offered our sincere congratulations. He and his wife still met, but only occasionally, as she had moved on to an even higher vibration.

Some husbands and wives stay very closely together in the Spirit World, whereas others go on their separate ways following their own interests, as often happens here. I am also asked - what about the problems of two or more spouses here on the earth - and the answer we have been given is that there are no problems over there. Many who have passed over previously will continue to go their own ways, and like the couple I have just mentioned, meet occasionally. Some, with nothing but resentment for their former partners, may not make contact again until that feeling has been resolved and removed. Others with deeper feelings of true love may link together as a group, irrespective of how many of each gender, and continue to work together.

As I relate in the notes about the Christmas Party sitting on 3rd January 1948, Dad Hudson's first wife, Hannah, materialized and personally thanked his present wife, Annie Hudson, for taking on the responsibilities of bringing up her five children. I'm sure they had no problems when they were all reunited over there, some years ago now.

Aunt Agg told us that there were times when she still operated as a medium in the Spirit World - to contact Spirit people who had progressed to those higher vibrations and were technically unable to lower their vibrations to get in touch with friends and relatives who had just passed over or were still even here on earth. This may seem rather strange, but it is no different from the way mediums operate here on the earth to contact our Spirit friends, whom they assure us, are only one step ahead - awaiting our 'catching up' when our time arrives.

I must repeat - the Spirit World is just as *real* to them as the Earth is to us, but on a higher, finer vibration. They certainly have their 'Halls of Learning' with the most comprehensive lists of subjects including the arts, music, philosophy, science, nature studies, spiritual advancement and all other matters of general interest. Spirit 'masters' from higher regions visit and give talks and lectures. There are vast libraries and musical concerts are readily available with, we are told, wonderful colours woven into the music.

However, if they feel the need for some privacy, especially in the early period of being in the Spirit World, they can have houses or cottages to their own designs. Their gardens and countryside include plants and flowers of such bright but delicate colours that we cannot even visualise them - they are so different and have a special 'pristine' character. If they so desire, people may also have their pets with them, which can be such a comfort in many cases.

In other words, you can do or have what you want so long as it is in harmony with your environment and your fellow beings. Those who feel the need can still have their cups of tea or glasses of ale for as long as they want such material 'comforts', but the majority soon realize such things are unnecessary in their new surroundings.

Many of Arthur Findlay's books, especially 'Where Two Worlds Meet', include similar reports through the mediumship of John Sloan, and I'm certain that many readers will have come across such corroborative testimony in other books, like 'Life in the World Unseen' by Anthony Borgia - well worth reading if you can obtain a copy. Neville Randall's book 'Life after Death', another excellent read, deals with a number of the 500 tapes recorded by George Woods and Betty Greene at special Leslie Flint direct voice séances in the 1950-70's.

In the Leslie Flint séances people from all stations of life on earth recounted their experiences in the Spirit World and they were all so different, many philosophical stories from learned people, with the majority, full of humour, telling of their everyday lives. For all of them it is a 'real' world, on a higher vibration, inhabited by hosts of Spirit people living the kinds of lives, which suits them individually - surprisingly, sometimes not unlike the kind of life they lived on the earth, if that is their wish. It is truly a *real world* full of boundless opportunities limited only by each individual's desires.

So open your minds to the Spirit World and think more deeply to prepare yourself for your transition whenever it may occur. When you are considering travelling to new places, especially abroad, I feel sure you try to find out as much as possible about your destination and the conditions of life in the country you are visiting. Such enquiries enable you to be prepared for your new surroundings and make life much more enjoyable, if only for those brief holiday visits.

When the move is permanent however, especially with emigration, we surely have to have much more detailed information to be ready to integrate into our new surroundings with the minimum of complications. Baden-Powell's motto - 'Be Prepared', is surely well worth putting into practice for the one journey, which is a certainty. Make it a happy and enjoyable journey to a welcoming and brighter destination.

Let Syd and Gladys' words, when they were being interviewed for the BBC broadcast, close this chapter. Chris asked them how they felt about dying now they were towards the end of their lives.

"I'm not afraid of anything", said Gladys, "We're not afraid to die. We understand you evolve to a high level but we don't know the details."

Syd added, "We just look at it philosophically, like saying we're going to Australia next year or the year after that. That's how we look at it. The knowledge of this removes any fear. Fear is a result of misunderstanding. We understand the general reception that you get. We know we are not wicked people. You go to a place very similar to this world so it's not a big shock to you. You meet a lot of people you know. Then gradually you become a citizen of the next world."

Thank you, friends, for helping so many understand this truth.

In Closing

In the 30 years, before moving to Spain when I gave my illustrated talks about the Circle I always invited questions and comments from the audience at the end of each talk. Unfortunately at the end of a book there can be no such 'open session' and further investigation is left in the hands of the reader.

For those readers wishing to investigate further, there will always be someone or some reliable and helpful organisation to turn to. 'Seek and ye shall find' is as applicable as ever and you could be pleasantly surprised by what you can discover in 'your own backyard'

What was witnessed in our Home Circle was undeniable *'living proof'* to all of those present, but can never *be proof to* anyone else - and I would never suggest it should be.

For you as the reader it can be nothing more than *evidence* - the strength of which is commensurate with the credibility of the witness - as with the jury in a Court of Law.

I trust I have impressed you as a genuine and honest witness- I have no reason whatsoever to be otherwise - but as Professor Fontana says - the final judgement is still yours. Accept only what appeals to your reasoning and current level of understanding, bearing in mind how our perception changes with increased knowledge.

I hope your knowledge has now increased, and what at the beginning of this book was almost unbelievable, may now be more acceptable to your reasoning. If not, all I ask is that you do not completely discard it, but tuck it away in your mind's filing system and allow it to come to fruition in the years ahead - either here or on the 'Other Side', which is the eventual destination of everyone, irrespective of their religious belief. This is the one certainty in this physical life.

Your personal proof may be years ahead, or just around the corner - so at all times keep an open mind ready to seize it when it presents itself- from however an expected or unpredictable source. Be sure you are ready for that propitious moment - a moment of indefinable understanding and enlightenment- an unforgettable moment to be forever treasured.

Thank you for your company on this very brief sojourn and though you may never have the thrill and privilege of meeting your Spirit loved ones face to face, as I did, - very few people do — always remember that they are around and amongst us, ever ready to make their presence felt when the opportunity arises. They are never more than a thought away.

May your journey in pursuit of Truth afford you as much joy as our journey has given to us.

"It is an old maxim of mine, that when you have excluded the impossible, whatever remains, however improbable, must be the Truth."

Sir Arthur Conan Doyle.

AFFADAVIT

Robin Hood's Bay
North Yorkshire

April 2003

SATURDAY NIGHT CLUB - HOME CIRCLE

We, the undersigned, are pleased to confirm in writing that we were two of the six founder members of the Saturday Night Club Home Circle, with the medium being Tom Harrison's mother, Mrs Minnie Harrison.

Our first sitting was on 6th April 1946 in our home in Acklam Road (later renamed as Burlam Road) Middlesbrough, where we sat weekly until August 1952 when we moved to Eastbourne Road and the sittings were then transferred to Tom and Doris Harrison's home in Oxford Road, Middlesbrough where they continued until Minnie Harrison's passing in 1958.

We saw Tom making notes after each sitting for the first two years and witnessed the Saturday Night Club phenomena, as detailed in Tom's book, including Telekinesis, Spirit lights, Spirit writing, Apports, Spirit voices through the trumpet and all the Ectoplasmic phenomena from Spirit hands to fully materialised Spirit people walking amongst us in a good red light. Apart from the very occasional absence due to sickness, we were present at all the sittings.

Sydney Shipman
Sydney Shipman

Gladys Shipman
Gladys Shipman

Eric Boyd
Eric Boyd
(Witness)

11th April 2003
(Date)

Reading on People and Topics included in the book
Many of these books are out of print but may be available from
second-hand specialists.

Alec Harris	..They Walked Among Us.- Louie Harris
Alfred Kitson ..	Alfred Kitson Autobiography
Anthony Borgia	Life in the World Unseen
	More About Life in the World Unseen
	Facts
	Heaven and Earth
Arthur Findlay ..	Where Two Worlds Meet
	Looking Back
	On the Edge of the Etheric
Baron Schrenck Notzing	The University of Spiritualism'-.Boddington
Ena Twigg ..	Ena Twigg, Medium(autobiography)
George Spriggs(Circle of light) ..	Cavalcade of Spirit..- Paul Miller
Gordon Higginson	On the Side of the Angels
Grace Rosher	.. Beyond the Horizon
Harris, Bertha ..	Battling Bertha by M. Leonard
Harry Edwards	Born to Heal (biography)- Paul Miller
Helen Duncan ..	The Story of Helen Duncan.- A. Crossley
..	Hellish Nell. Malcolm Gaskill
Helen Greaves ..	The Wheel of Eternity;
	Testimony of Light
Hunter Selkirk ..	Listen My Son-Harry Emerson(private pub)
Jack Webber ..	The Mediumship of JackWebber.- H.Edwards
Katie Halliwell ..	Trance and Physical Mediumship Experiences
	with Stewart Alexander. Available privately from:
	The Alexander Project, 85 Alexandra Rd, Hull,HU5 2NX
Leslie Flint ..	Voices in the Dark
Maurice Barbanell	This is Spiritualism
	Power of the Spirit
Neville Randall ..	Life After Death (Flint -direct voices)
Roy Dixon Smith	New Light on Survival
Stephen Turoff ..	Seven Steps to Eternity
	Stephen Turoff, Psychic Surgeon.- G. Solomon
Stewart Alexander	(see Katie Halliwell)
William Crookes, Sir	Researches

On Phenomena
Apports,Trance,   -The Power of Spirit- Maurice Barbanell
Ectoplasm, experiments with —WJ Crawford/ Baron Schrenck
Notzing - see - 'The University of Spiritualism'- Harry Boddington

Other Sources

These are all current at the time of writing:-
Arthur Findlay College (for advancement of Psychic Science)
Stansted Hall, Stansted, Essex CM24 8UD
Tel:01279 813636.   afc@snu.org.uk

The Spiritualist National Union
Redwoods, Stansted Hall, Stansted, Essex CM24 8UD
Tel: 01279 816363.   snu@snu.org.uk   www.snu.org.uk
Psychic News (a weekly newspaper est. 1932)
Psychic Press; The Coach House, Stansted Hall, Stansted
Tel: 01279 817050.   pn@snu.org.uk

College of Psychic Studies
16, Queensbury Place, London SW7 2EB
Tel: 0207 589 3292

Churches Fellowship for Psychical/Spiritual Studies (CFPSS)
The Rural Workshop, South Road, North Somercotes
Nr Louth, Lincolnshire LN11 7PT
Tel: 0507 358 845   gensec@cfpss.freeserve.co.uk
The Christian Parapsychologist and *The Quarterly Review*

Society for Psychical Research (SPR)
49, Marloes Road, London W8 6LA
Tel: 0207 937 8984   www.spr.ac.uk   uksociety@aol.com
Journal for the SPR and *The Paranormal Review*

Web sites for good articles and photographs
www.cfpf.org.uk   - Campaign for Philosophical Freedom
www.survivalafterdeath.org/home.htm
                    - International Survivalist Society.
http://nsac.phenomena.com - American Spiritualist site
www.medium2000.org -Fellowship of Spiritual Truth

Also available from SNPP:-
'Visitors from the Other Side' - 60 min. Video/DVD of Tom
talking about the Saturday Night Club plus interviews with
others who also sat.
 Christmas Party Sitting – 90 min. cassette tape of the sitting on
5th January 1954.   Contact:-   lifeafterdeath@bigfoot.com